Pierre Sauvage
How They Entertain
At Home with the Tastemakers

Pierre Sauvage
How They Entertain
At Home with the Tastemakers

Text **Cédric Saint André Perrin**   Photography **Ambroise Tézenas**

FLAMMARION

Contents

FOREWORD *Carolina Irving* 6
INTRODUCTION *Pierre Sauvage* 9
Filipa de Abreu *10*
Aurélie Bidermann *24*
Isabelle de Borchgrave *38*
Sophie Bouilhet-Dumas *56*
Muriel Brandolini *70*
Flore de Brantes *84*
Brigitte Bury Dervault and Maurice Dervault *100*
Françoise Dumas *114*
Nathalie Farman-Farma *130*
Laura Gonzalez *146*
Olympia and Ariadne Irving *164*
Isabelle Moltzer *176*
Pascale Mussard *194*
Franz Potisek *206*
Rebecca de Ravenel *224*
Remy Renzullo *236*
Caroline Sarkozy *250*
Pierre Sauvage *264*
Scott Stover *288*
Sabine Van Vlaenderen Badinter *304*
INDEX OF RECIPES *319*

Foreword

Interiors and entertaining: two of my favorite things reunited in one book! What could be better?

Pierre invites us to enter these wonderful houses, each with its own distinct personality and style.

This is very much a book about individuality, particularly when it comes to entertaining, which is indeed an art, and one that I'm happy to see is becoming an obsession with everyone.

There is huge pleasure in being a guest, but equally in being a host or hostess, from the sense of anticipation and the rediscovered rituals to the desire to make your friends happy. For a few hours, time is suspended and everything is perfect.

So I'll sit back, open this book, and let myself be a guest. I'll look closely at how flowers are arranged and tables are set, and I'll fantasize about trying the recipes—armchair traveling at its best.

CAROLINA IRVING

FACING PAGE
Pierre Sauvage's three pedigree shih tzus stand guard on an Empire-style banquette in the entrance hall of his manor house in the Perche region.

Introduction

To draw up a table plan, you need a dash of psychology, a measure of intuition, and a pinch of recklessness. The art of seating your guests lies in ensuring that they share more than just a meal: it is about creating stimulating conversations that may lead to new friendships, projects, plans for life—or maybe even for later that evening. At the very least, you aim to create a moment for friends to come together around a delicious meal, with an added element of surprise, to raise adrenaline levels, since guests do not know who they will be sitting next to until they come to the table. The same could be said of this book, which I hope will prove to be as entertaining as it is inspiring.

Within its pages, I invite you to meet some of those who are dear to me—or who inspire me—and whose talents and *art de vivre* I would like to share with you here. I therefore asked Cédric Saint André Perrin to join me in this venture, to sketch pen portraits of the hosts and hostesses featured here. With another friend, the talented photographer Ambroise Tézenas, we set off to meet prominent creative individuals in London and Paris, Comporta, Portugal, and the Luberon, southern France. Opening wide the doors of their apartments, villas, châteaux, and family estates, they have given us the opportunity to capture the distinctive atmosphere of each interior in a handful of images. They have created their most delightful table settings for us, and have even entrusted us with their favorite recipes, with which they regale their guests. And—as you will see—hearty eating and insider tips win out over complicated cuisine, every time!

Some of the hosts and hostesses in this book work in the world of fashion, others in interior design or contemporary art. As styles and generations mix and mingle, overlap and intersect, the only constant in these pages is the flair with which they shape their lifestyles as extensions of their personalities. Each of them welcomes their friends in their own way. The formality of the past is replaced by a tremendous freedom of style. Whether designing a living space or organizing a party, everyone has their own approach, their own treasured recipes, their own special knack. Contained within these pages is a cornucopia of great ideas.

PIERRE SAUVAGE

FACING PAGE
A meticulously folded collection of napkins—custom-made or vintage—enables Pierre Sauvage to mix and match his table settings.

Filipa de Abreu

She has lived in Lisbon, Athens, London, Paris, and Los Angeles, and she spends a lot of time in India, which doubtless accounts for the bohemian exuberance of her style. Filipa de Abreu, a fashion and interior design consultant who skips with ease from one language or creative venture to another, welcomes us in Comporta.

"I wanted a setting that was simple, easy, and family-oriented: we have five children and two dogs, so we can do without stressing over anything fragile in the house," she says with a laugh. "It's a place where life is easy and relaxed, where we and the children can have our friends to stay. There's nothing fancy about the way the house is decorated, but it's really welcoming. It's a happy place, and above all it's in harmony with the unspoiled nature all around us." A paradise set between the ocean, rice fields, sand dunes, and pine forests, Comporta offers the luxury of surroundings that are untouched and authentic, where you can enjoy the present moment to the full. For many years a secret known only to a few regular visitors, the region has become a veritable haven for those who are fortunate enough to be here.

There are no night clubs, beach bars, or trendy restaurants: Comporta is not the new Ibiza. People have fun, of course, but they do so in private, with friends. No one is better at setting a table under an umbrella pine and bringing together a group of good friends than Filipa de Abreu. "Dressing a table is my love language, my way of showing my guests how much I care. Their presence makes all the effort involved worthwhile! A fun dinner is a party that guests never want to leave." Her secret for a successful meal? "Lots to drink," she laughs. "Since my cooking skills are slightly limited, I make sure my friends have had plenty to drink before they even sit down to eat. That way, no one will notice whether or not I've burnt the main course!"

Filipa de Abreu's art of entertaining is her response to a very personal vision: "I respond to beauty, and I appreciate unpretentious elegance and comfort. Good friends, family, music, and lots of laughter—this is what gives me life!" This is what shines through on her Instagram feed, where she shares her day-to-day partnerships with luxury labels, between event planning and original marketing strategies. Digital marketing, image strategy, and PR are her special skills, all with a generous dash of style. Let's just say she's an ambassador for online chic, her territory of expression.

FACING PAGE
Filipa de Abreu picks the flowers of the flamboyant tree in her garden in Portugal.

FACING PAGE, ABOVE, RIGHT, AND PAGES 14–15
A shady terrace, like an outdoor living space opening onto the garden, makes an inviting spot for reading and daydreaming. Here, life is lived outside as much as inside.

Russian Salad

Ingredients (serves 4)

4 eggs
4 potatoes
⅓ cup (2 oz./60 g) green vegetables
(green beans, petits pois, zucchini)
4 carrots
8 cherry tomatoes, halved
Fines herbes
4 tbsp mayonnaise
8 green olives
Radishes, cut into flowers
Viola flowers, to decorate (optional)
Salt and freshly ground black pepper

Method

Hard-boil the eggs and let them cool.
Boil and drain the potatoes, green vegetables, and carrots.
When cool, cube the potatoes, slice the green beans, zucchini, and carrots, and mix with the petits pois, halved cherry tomatoes, and *fines herbes*.
Season with salt and pepper and add lots of mayonnaise.
Peel and chop the eggs and add them with the green olives.
Decorate with a few radishes cut into flowers and viola flowers, if using.
Refrigerate for around an hour.
Serve well chilled.

BELOW
Banquette seating upholstered in a geometric motif beside the flamboyant tree in the garden.

PAGES 18–19
Filipa's table: the motifs and colors evoke
the sea and showcase Portuguese craftsmanship.

ABOVE AND LEFT
A wall filled with a collection of exotic trophies,
cushions with humorous messages in cross-stitch,
and rattan furniture all conspire to create
a bohemian ambience.

FACING PAGE
A collection of shells and corals displayed
in a Caliansi cabinet, flanked by a pair of rococo
stucco columns.

FACING PAGE
A collection of straw boaters, wide-brimmed hats, and Panama hats makes a decorative feature in the hall.

RIGHT, TOP
Bohemian minimalism under the eaves.

RIGHT, BOTTOM
A clutch of raffia bags and totes.

Aurélie Bidermann

Her eponymous jewelry brand, which she is no longer a part of, was launched in the early 2000s. Today, Madame Aurélie Bidermann continues to design not only jewelry, but also creations for the home, through a series of collaborations.

"I've always been passionate about the arts, in all their forms, as my tastes are quite eclectic," declares this native Parisienne. "I can be inspired by a trip to Italy or a flea-market find. I'm open to a host of different things." Since her parents were collectors of art nouveau, Aurélie Bidermann could easily have envisaged a career as an auctioneer. In fact, she studied history of art in Paris and London, and began her career at Sotheby's New York, before she headed to India and succumbed to the magic of gemstones. So then it was off to Antwerp to specialize in gemology and train in technical drawing. She began making jewelry, and in 2004 she launched her own business. Her first collection, called Charms, featured lucky charm bracelets and necklaces, and would be followed by many more wonderful creations. The brand still exists, but she is no longer involved. Nowadays, she expresses her creativity through partnerships ranging from jewelry to tableware and home décor. For Christofle, she has designed her Babylone collection, combining dining, home decoration, and jewelry, and based on the recurring motif of curvaceous, silver-plated braids that can be worn as a cuff or used as a bowl. The collection borrows its pared-back lines and graphic elegance from the aesthetic of art deco, but with a femininity, softness, and generosity that are all its own.

Needless to say, this dinner service is to be found gracing Aurélie Bidermann's own table. "I like to entertain my friends. It could be just four guests who come regularly to eat in the kitchen, or eight in the dining room, when I mix different groups of friends. I vary the menu according to whether my guests are vegetarians, vegans, or carnivores. These days you have to be flexible," she laughs. "But mostly it's fish, which suits most people. My own preference would be for Mediterranean cuisine, but I'm naturally very open-minded." This openness can be seen even in the layout of her Left Bank interior, with its atmosphere of comfortable elegance. Here, an armoire by Jacques Adnet (1900–1984) sits alongside travel mementoes and fine art photographs. Just a stone's throw away lies the Jardin du Luxembourg, where Aurélie Bidermann loves to go for walks with her daughter. A tranquil life but a full one.

FACING PAGE
Aurélie Bidermann at her window, wearing the solid silver cuffs from her Babylone collection for Christofle.

ABOVE, LEFT
In the living room, a vintage coffee table with a rattan-covered base and white lacquer top.

ABOVE, RIGHT
Shells, pebbles, and bouquets of dried grasses decorate the large coffee table.

FACING PAGE
On the console table is a small porcelain vase designed by Aurélie Bidermann for Christofle. On the wall above, a Ginkgo wall sconce by Tommasso Barbi.

PAGES 28–29
In the living room, shades of pale pink, white, and gold create a soft, warm atmosphere.

FACING PAGE
A painting by Tony Cox hangs above a row of colored glass apothecary jars.

BELOW
Beside a Jacques Adnet mirror armoire in the living room, a small chair with a Plexiglas base by Éric Chevalier.

PAGES 32–33
Plates, candle holders, tumblers, and napkin rings from the Babylone collection for Christofle.

Soupe au Potimarron (Squash Soup)

Ingredients (serves 4)

6 red kuri squash, 4 of equal size
3 carrots
Small piece fresh ginger
Salt and freshly ground pepper

Method

Choose four red kuri squash the same size, and slice off their tops to form lids. Use a large spoon to hollow out the insides, removing the seeds and a little of the flesh. Set aside.
Chop the two remaining squash and the carrots into small pieces and grate the ginger. Put them all in a saucepan, cover with water, and simmer over a low heat until soft.
Remove any excess water if the consistency seems too liquid, and blend until smooth. Season to taste.
Carefully pour the soup into the squash shells.
Serve hot.

Leek Quiche with Flowers

Ingredients (serves 4)

3 leeks
Butter, for sautéing
1 pack round ready-rolled butter puff pastry
3 eggs
Scant cup (200 ml) crème fraîche
Nutmeg
¾ cup (3 ½ oz./100 g) Gruyère, grated
Edibles flower and green vegetables, to decorate (optional)
Salt and freshly ground black pepper

Method

Preheat the oven to 400°F (180°C/Gas Mark 6).
Slice the leeks and sauté them in butter until soft. Set aside.
Line a tart pan with the pastry, lifting and pinching together the edges of the pastry to form a raised crust.
Spread the leeks evenly over the pastry.
Beat the eggs with the crème fraîche. Add nutmeg and season with salt and pepper.
Pour this mixture over the leeks and sprinkle with the grated Gruyère.
Bake in the oven for 45 minutes. When cool, decorate with edible flowers and green vegetables if desired.

FACING PAGE AND ABOVE
Collages of images from magazines and children's paintings decorate the walls of Aurélie's daughter's bedroom, as well as the "look wall" of her own studio in her Paris apartment.

RIGHT
Shamrocks on the bed linen by Porthault blend with the paisley motif of the linen wallpaper.

Isabelle de Borchgrave

The Belgian artist Isabelle de Borchgrave, famed for her intricate works crafted in paper, lives and works in a colorful studio in the heart of Brussels. Together with her husband, Werner, and with the help of their architect friends Claire Bataille and Paul Ibens, she has transformed this 16,000-square-foot (1,500-square-meter) former garage into a space that is at once a studio, home, and gallery.

This is where Isabelle de Borchgrave, with a team of eight assistants, creates spectacular costumes out of paper, reproducing silks, embroidered cottons, lace, and velvets, as well as vases and jewelry displayed in cardboard armoires. She started this work in the mid-1990s, after a visit to the Metropolitan Museum of Art inspired her to create a collection of historic garments: "I love working with paper, a multifaceted material, to make sculptural objects, miniature architectural structures, and costumes. Each piece captures a moment in history." Her endlessly varied output also embraces garden furniture, tableware, and cushions inspired by her painted work.

In her living room, lit by a huge glass partition leading to one of the building's terraces, past and present mingle together to create an ambience that is as warmly welcoming as it is eclectic. Objects from around the world set up a dialogue with her own works, as well as some baroque-era pieces including eighteenth-century columns from a Salzburg pharmacy. This is where she likes to entertain, keeping things simple and relaxed. "We have lunch here with my coworkers, clients, and friends who happen to be passing; it's friendly and uncomplicated. Everyone mingles and it's really nice. In the evening, I like to dress tables with candles and flowers. Sometimes we go upstairs afterward to the studio, where one of our friends will play the piano. Space and music are my luxuries. At my private views there can be as many as six hundred people! My studio makes it possible for me to change the format for my parties."

Outside, a pool with koi carp and plant-filled terraces are a charming contrast to the minimalism of the building's architecture. Isabelle de Borchgrave has chosen the trees and shrubs—ginkgo, crab apple, dogwood, and hornbeam—for their shapes and colors and the way their hues change with the seasons, creating a harmonious world of plants. The welcoming space she has created here reflects her love of travel and her passion for art and nature.

FACING PAGE
Isabelle de Borchgrave in her Brussels studio, at work on a paper découpage composition.

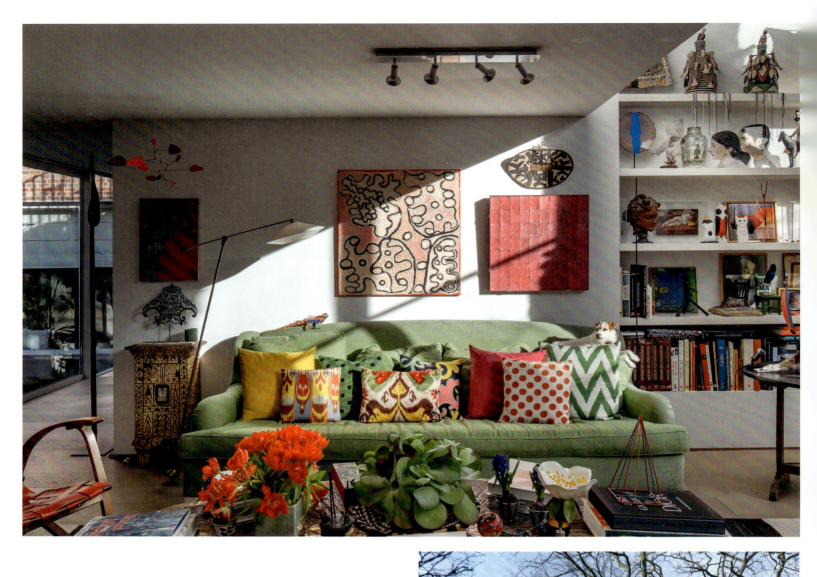

PAGES 40–41, ABOVE, FACING PAGE, AND PAGES 44–45
True to her passion for bohemian style, Isabelle mixes and matches motifs and color palettes in the various living spaces scattered through her spacious home.

RIGHT
Glazed doors beneath a semicircular window lead into the living room.

Sea Bass Ceviche

Ingredients (serves 4)

5 ½ oz. (160 g) sea bass fillets
Juice of 4 limes
Juice of 2 lemons
1 red onion
1 or 2 chiltepin chilis
1 cucumber
1 punnet cherry tomatoes

Fresh ginger
Cilantro
Dill
Olive oil
Salt and freshly ground black pepper

Method

Slice the sea bass into thin strips. In a dish, mix the strips with the juice of the limes and lemons. Cover with plastic wrap and refrigerate for 15–20 minutes.

Meanwhile, finely chop the red onion and chilis. Peel the cucumber, remove the seeds, and cut into small cubes. Quarter the cherry tomatoes.

Grate the ginger. Pull the cilantro leaves off the stems and chop the dill.

Remove the sea bass from the refrigerator. Season with salt and pepper. Add the finely chopped chilis and onion, grated ginger, cucumber, and tomatoes. Gently mix together.

To serve, garnish with the cilantro, dill, and a drizzle of olive oil.

RIGHT
In the dining area, a sculptural and oversized paper chandelier hangs over a matching pair of verre églomisé tables.

Orange and Mint Salad

Ingredients (serves 4)

8 oranges
Cinnamon
Bunch of fresh mint

Method

Peel the oranges with a knife and cut them into segments.

Sprinkle with cinnamon and add the chopped mint leaves to serve.

ABOVE
The table decorations invite guests into a colorful, quirky world.

PAGES 52–53, FACING PAGE, ABOVE, AND RIGHT
A multitalented artist who has chosen paper as her medium, Isabelle de Borchgrave makes dresses, printed fabrics, and artworks, all displayed in the house-studio that also serves as her gallery.

Sophie Bouilhet-Dumas

Sophie Bouilhet-Dumas, creator of the Mira Stella jewelry label, throws open the doors of her family home, L'Ange Volant, a neoclassical masterpiece designed for her paternal grandparents by the Italian architect and designer Gio Ponti (1891–1979).

"I grew up here, and I come back for weekends and vacations. My sisters and I have undertaken major works to bring the place back to life," declares Sophie Bouilhet-Dumas, who in 2018 helped to curate the first retrospective devoted to Gio Ponti, mounted by the Musée des Arts Décoratifs in Paris. Built in 1928 on the hillside in Garches, near the Saint-Cloud golf course, this beautiful residence, with its light, fresh hues, was designed by the Italian master architect down to its finest details, from the door handles to the sculptures on the façade, not forgetting the spectacular metalwork of the banisters on the main stair.

The hall ceiling is designed as a trompe-l'œil canopy, a theatrical touch featuring cartouches topped by diminutive French and Italian flags and containing the paired profiles of her parents, Tony and Carla Bouilhet. Flanking the hall on one side is a salon and library, and on the other a dining room where Sophie Bouilhet-Dumas loves to entertain: "The arts of the table are an obsession for me—something that runs in the family, in a way. I'm very receptive to anything that can make daily life more beautiful. I find the gestures and rituals of meals fascinating."

Now that the villa has been restored to its former glory, Sophie Bouilhet-Dumas is promoting L'Ange Volant through a program of exhibitions, location filming, and events. A longstanding artistic consultant for prominent names in tableware, including Paul Smith, Hermès, and Thomas Goode & Co, over the years she has also discovered a passion for gardens. Her love of nature led her to enlist the help of the English botanist Mark Brown in laying out wildflower meadows around the family's Normandy farmhouse, interspersed with flowerbeds designed to offer views over the nearby Alabaster Coast. The gardens in turn inspired her Mira Stella jewelry line, transforming life-size gold reproductions of sea kale seeds, hydrangea petals, and orache seeds into rings, brooches, and pendants.

FACING PAGE
Sophie Bouilhet-Dumas on the staircase with wrought-iron balustrades designed by Gio Ponti and made by Christofle.

BELOW
Above the front door, a gilded metal angel set in a tondo holds aloft a maquette of the Flying Angel, emblem of the house.

RIGHT
The villa's garden façade.

BELOW
A silver-plated tea and coffee service designed
by Lino Sabattini for Christofle in 1957.

FACING PAGE
In the living room, a suite of walnut burr furniture.
The design of the stair balustrade mirrors
the cartouches on the ceiling.

FACING PAGE AND ABOVE
Sophie Bouilhet-Dumas likes to compose table settings with plates and glasses that subtly echo the colors of the flowers freshly picked from her garden.

Tiramisu

Ingredients (serves 6–8)

6 eggs
1 ⅓ cups (7 oz./200 g) demerara sugar
2 sachets vanilla sugar
2 cups (1 lb. 2 oz./500 g) mascarpone
48 lady fingers or boudoir biscuits
3 cups (750 ml) very strong unsweetened black coffee
Scant ½ cup (1 ¾ oz./50 g) unsweetened cocoa powder

Method

Separate the egg yolks from the whites.

Beat the yolks with the demerara sugar and vanilla sugar until pale. Beat in the mascarpone.

Whip up the egg whites until stiff, then, using a spatula, carefully fold them into the mixture. Set aside.

Dip the lady fingers in the coffee and use them to line the base of a round dish.

Cover the lady fingers with a layer of mascarpone cream, then repeat, alternating layers of lady fingers and cream. Finish with a layer of cream. Sprinkle with cocoa powder.

Refrigerate for at least 4 hours before serving.

BELOW
Sunlight floods the dining room, dominated by a 1940s chandelier by Gio Ponti for Venini.

FACING PAGE
On the mezzanine overlooking the living room sits an office space with a 1950s desk by Gio Ponti, as well as his famous Superleggera chair.

BELOW
The desk in one of the bedrooms, overlooking the trees in the garden. On the wall, an arrow candelabra, a nuptial symbol designed by Gio Ponti for the wedding of Tony Bouilhet to Carla Borletti.

LEFT, TOP AND BOTTOM
The hand-painted ceramic tiles in the bathrooms were designed in the late 1950s for Gio Ponti's own family apartment in Milan.

FACING PAGE
Against the gray-green marmorino walls of the entrance hall hangs a brass arrow wall sconce designed by Gio Ponti.

Muriel Brandolini

A fascinating and galvanizing figure, Muriel Brandolini was born in Montpellier to a Vietnamese father and a mother of Venezuelan descent, and grew up in Saigon, Vietnam, and Martinique, before coming to study in Paris at the age of fifteen. She arrived in New York in 1979, and went on to work at Italian *Vogue*, before turning to interior design.

It was through decorating her New York apartment that this self-taught designer first garnered attention. Since then she has devoted her talents to a handpicked client list. "The choice is reciprocal," she explains. "It's all about mutual appreciation and understanding. There's something of the therapist in the role I play, helping people create spaces that will bring them serenity, restfulness, and privacy on a daily basis." Her cosmopolitan background has left an unmistakable mark on her exotic sensibility and eclectic imagination. Famed for her use of color, Muriel Brandolini excels in creating tonal compositions that are delicate and dreamlike. But there is nothing retro about her work: she has a gift for bringing contemporary creations, by Hervé Van der Straeten or Martin Szekely, head-to-head with baroque or Asian pieces, like the spectacular pagoda daybed in the living room of her Paris pied-à-terre.

While she divides her time between New York and the Hamptons, her heart still remains in the French capital: "It's in Paris that I hunt down my treasures: antiques at Drouot, design in the galleries. And I try out everything at home, here in Paris. Later on, my finds might travel on to other places. All through my life I have never parted with a piece, they move with me from one house to the next; sometimes I put them in storage and rediscover them at a later date—differently, in another way." Muriel Brandolini's approach to interior decoration is intuitive and spontaneous. "I don't overthink what I do," she insists. "I just do it, and it works!"

She also enjoys entertaining in her Left Bank apartment: "Paris is so different from New York: here people come at eight and may not leave before two in the morning. In America it's strictly from seven to ten: those are the rules! Conversation is freer in France and everything is less formal. We have our way of doing things, my husband Nuno and I. I dress the table and he does the cooking. I pay particular attention to the flowers. In fact, whenever I finish a house for a client, I show the maid how to create flower arrangements that match the ambience of the space. The ready-made bouquets that you can buy from florists aren't always the most appropriate."

FACING PAGE
Muriel Brandolini reclines with a book on the pagoda daybed that stands in the center of the library in her Paris pied-à-terre.

ABOVE
Beside the pagoda daybed, a bronze table by Michele Oka Doner and an unusual nineteenth-century giltwood armchair.

FACING PAGE
On the library wall, an antique Venetian mirror with a frame of glass palms.

PAGES 74–75, ABOVE, AND FACING PAGE
The dining room walls are hung with a Holland & Sherry fabric, the ceiling light and wall sconces are by Hervé Van der Straeten, and the table, chairs, and tableware are all vintage.

Blanquette de Veau

Ingredients (serves 4)

2 lb. 3 oz. (1 kg) shoulder of veal, boned and cut into 2 in. (5 cm) cubes
1 cube vegetable stock
3 leeks, green part only
1 red onion, peeled
Bouquet garni
4 carrots, sliced on an angle
3 leeks, white part only, cut into 2 in. (5 cm) pieces
6 small turnips, peeled and halved
1 bunch green asparagus, stalks peeled
14 oz. (400 g) button mushrooms, peeled and quartered
3 tbsp crème fraîche
Zest of 2 limes
White rice, to serve
Salt and black peppercorns

FOR THE SAUCE
Butter, for sautéing
2 white onions, finely sliced
2 shallots, finely sliced
A little veal stock
Salt and freshly ground black pepper

FOR THE ROUX
$2/3$ stick (2 $1/2$ oz./75 g) butter
$1/2$ cup (2 $1/2$ oz./75 g) flour
A little veal stock
Salt and freshly ground black pepper

Method

Place the veal in a medium-sized rondeau pan, cover with the vegetable stock, and bring to a simmer. Add the green part of the leeks and the red onion. Season generously with salt and black peppercorns. Add the bouquet garni.

While the veal is cooking, start preparing the sauce. Sauté the white onions and shallots in butter until very soft. Add a little veal stock and season with salt and pepper. It should look like a nice jammy mixture, but take care not to allow the onions to color: you need to keep everything as white as possible. Remove from the heat and set aside.

To make the roux, gently melt the butter in a skillet and add the flour, stirring constantly to prevent the mixture from taking on any color. Cook for about 5 minutes or until the flour smell is gone. Add a little veal stock, stirring constantly for a smooth consistency. Season with salt and pepper. Remove from the heat and set aside.

Remove the leeks, onion, and bouquet garni from the veal pot and replace them with the carrots, whites of leeks, turnips, and asparagus. These are the vegetables you will serve with the veal, so take care not to overcook them.

In a skillet, melt the butter and sauté the mushrooms, taking care not to let them color. Season with salt and pepper. When they have softened, add the crème fraîche and lime zest.

While the vegetables are cooking with the veal, blend the onion and shallot sauce mixture with the roux. Gradually add this to the veal pot through a fine-mesh sieve to thicken the blanquette. Remove from the heat.

The final consistency should be a pale-colored veal stew, not too thick, but with a good amount of sauce.

To serve, arrange the veal, vegetables, and mushrooms on a dish, mixing the meat with the vegetables. Pour over a thin blanket of sauce while still leaving the veal and vegetables visible.

Serve with white rice.

PAGES 80–81
A silver and porcelain chandelier repurposed as a set of flower vases.

Îles Flottantes (Floating Islands)

Ingredients (serves 4)

FOR THE CUSTARD
Generous 1 cup (500 ml) reduced-fat milk
1 vanilla pod
6 egg yolks
⅓ cup (2 ½ oz./75 g) superfine sugar

FOR THE MERINGUES
6 egg whites
½ cup (3 ½ oz./100 g) superfine sugar
Pinch salt

FOR THE CARAMEL
½ cup (3 ½ oz./100 g) superfine sugar

Method

To make the custard, bring the milk to a simmer with the vanilla pod, opened and with the seeds scraped out. When it has simmered, set it aside for 10 minutes to allow the vanilla to release its aroma. Strain through a sieve.

In a bowl, whisk together the egg yolks and sugar until pale. Add the milk, whisking constantly, then pour into a saucepan. Cook over a low heat, stirring constantly in a figure eight with a wooden spoon.

The custard is ready when it reaches 180°F (83°C), or when any froth has disappeared from the surface and the mixture coats the back of the spoon. Allow to cool in the refrigerator.

To make the meringues, fill a large saucepan with water and bring to a simmer.

Using an electric whisk, beat the egg whites with a pinch of salt. When they begin to stiffen, add the sugar and continue whisking for a few minutes.

When the water reaches a gentle simmer, use a slotted spoon to divide the meringue mixture into six portions, or shape it into six balls between two tablespoons, and place them in the water. Cook for a few seconds on both sides, then remove from the water with a slotted spoon and place on a wire rack to drain. When all the meringues are cooked, arrange them on top of the custard in the bowl. Refrigerate until ready to serve.

To make the caramel, heat the sugar (with no water) over a low heat until it melts and turns a lovely amber color. Pour slowly from a tablespoon on to a sheet of parchment paper, forming fine strands into nests, then leave to cool before gently peeling off. To serve, pour custard into each bowl, add a floating island, then arrange the caramel decoration on top.

Flore de Brantes

Flore de Brantes divides her time between Paris and the Château du Fresne, her ancestral home in the Loir-et-Cher region, a handsome neoclassical building near Tours that she is striving to bring back to life. Not content with restoring her château to its former glory, she pours her energies above all into adapting it to suit her own unconventional lifestyle and that of her two sons, as well as for her tenants.

"The house is big, it needs to be lived in; I love entertaining here at weekends," declares Flore de Brantes. "To this end, I've developed my own personal protocol: on Friday evening, a dinner to welcome guests in the servants' dining hall—there aren't really any staff left, but there's still a lovely vaulted dining hall. On Saturday we have lunch in the grounds or beside the pool—if the weather's fine enough, that is! And in the evening we have a grand dinner. For these I bring out the formal dinner service and silverware and make lovely flower arrangements. I always set the table earlier in the week, so that I can really enjoy my guests." She regales her friends with dishes based on vegetables from the kitchen garden and offers them fruit from the orchard. The cheeses and wines are invariably from the region. As an aperitif, she serves her "Le FloreLess" cocktail, based on champagne and peach juice, with a splash of vodka and a rose from the garden as a *touillette* or stirrer—an idea first thought up by Colin Field, the legendary bartender of the Bar Hemingway at the Ritz Paris, now dedicated to the most modern of châtelaines.

After a long career as a gallerist in the decorative arts, Flore de Brantes changed direction to become a rural entrepreneur: "I look after my farms, forests, and gardens, which boast over a thousand dahlias that are my pride and joy. I love making bouquets!" Some of the outbuildings are rented out to Parisians looking for a weekend getaway forty-five minutes from the capital, others are available on Airbnb for short stays, while the château itself is available to businesses as a venue for team-building sessions with a difference for their employees or clients.

In order to do this, Flore de Brantes has been busily restoring this eighteenth-century manor house. The slate roof has been refurbished, and bathrooms and central heating have been installed: "I show my spanking new radiators off to my visitors with great pride; they leave my visitors cold, but they warm my heart. And in the winter it's not just my heart!" The Savonnerie carpets have been also cleaned and mended to go with the new curtains and wall coverings. Here and there a few pieces of a more recent vintage have sprung up, such as the 1950s metal palm trees. "The main thing is that nothing should look new: on no account must anyone think an interior designer had been anywhere near the place!"

FACING PAGE
Flore de Brantes on the main staircase of the château, an armful of cuttings from the garden over her shoulder, ready to arrange the flowers for the bedrooms.

FACING PAGE
The château's neoclassical architecture reflected in an expanse of still water.

BELOW
View down the enfilade of reception rooms.

PAGES 88–89
The library, with its delicately carved wood paneling.

FACING PAGE
Above the Directoire-style dining room furniture, the ceiling is decorated with a surrealist fresco commissioned by Flore de Brantes from the Spanish artist Ignacio Goitia.

ABOVE, RIGHT, AND PAGES 92–93
Silverware, porcelain, endive leaves, cabbages, and boughs of roses from the château gardens mingle to create a romantic table decoration.

"Le Floreless" Cocktail, invented by Colin Field at the Bar Hemingway, Ritz Paris

Ingredients (serves 1)

2 ¾ tsp (40 ml) Pêche du Verger peach juice
4 tsp (20 ml) vodka
Sant ½ cup (100 ml) champagne or Triple Zéro from the Domaine de la Taille aux Loups
Garden roses

Method

Pour the peach juice and vodka into a cocktail shaker and add ice. Shake. Strain into a champagne flute.

Add the champagne or Triple Zéro, pouring slowly to keep the fizz. Stir very gently.

Using a pin, attach a rose to the glass.

Drink while still very chilled.

Rhubarb and Strawberry Meringue Pie

Ingredients (serves 4)

FOR THE SHORTCRUST PASTRY
⅔ cup (2 ½ oz./75 g) flour
⅓ stick (1 ⅓ oz./35 g) butter
1 ½ tbsp water
Pinch salt

FOR THE FILLING
1 cup (250 ml) light cream
1 egg
1 ½ tbsp sugar
Heaped tbsp flour

FOR THE FRUIT GARNISH
1 lb. 2 oz. (500 g) rhubarb
7 oz. (200 g) strawberries

FOR THE MERINGUE
2 egg whites
⅓ cup (2 ½ oz./75 g) superfine sugar

Method

Preheat the oven to 400°F (180°C/Gas Mark 6). Peel the rhubarb and slice into small pieces.

To make the pastry, mix the flour and salt and rub in the butter, cut into small pieces, then use the heel of your hand to work the mixture. Add the water, knead lightly, and shape into a ball.

Roll out the pastry dough with a rolling pin. Line a tart pan with the pastry and prick the base with a fork.

To make the filling, whisk together the cream, egg, sugar, and flour in a bowl. Arrange the rhubarb pieces on the pastry and pour the mixture over.

Bake in the oven for around 30 minutes.

Remove the tart from the oven and allow to cool.

To make the meringue, beat the egg whites, gently folding in the sugar until they form stiff peaks.

Place the meringue mixture in a pastry bag and pipe rosettes on top of the tart.

Use a blowtorch to gently toast the meringue.

Hull the strawberries and arrange between the meringue rosettes.

ABOVE
A mural decoration by Zuber in one of the bedrooms.

FACING PAGE
A canopy crowns the bathtub, with its commanding views over the gardens.

FACING PAGE
Hendricks the labrador relaxing on a *lit à la polonaise* set in an alcove.

ABOVE AND LEFT
Views of the gardens and a guest bedroom, all imbued with a romantic feel.

Brigitte Bury Dervault and Maurice Dervault

She enjoys setting appealing tables under the pergola, coordinating her table decorations with the colors of her dishes. He is forever rethinking the contours of his garden, planting one day, brush-cutting the next. Together, they have made Le Domaine des Sources into their own Garden of Eden.

"A house is a little like a snapshot in time. Ours is made up of memories and projects. It's like us, it brings us together," says Brigitte Bury Dervault. Having worked for many years at *Vogue*, first as a stylist and later as editor, and after some time at the helm of *Maison & Jardin* magazine, before breathing new life into Baccarat, she is passionate about design. It was she who conceived the idea of transforming the former Noailles residence on Place des États-Unis into a palace filled with contemporary crystal, under the aegis of Philippe Starck. She also supported the jeweler Elie Top as her career took off. Not to be outdone, her husband, Maurice, with his many years experience in luxury manufacturing, is no less appreciative of good design.

Following the coronavirus pandemic, the couple moved definitively to this fine eighteenth-century building in the heart of the Luberon in the South of France, where they now juggle the whims of nature with the upkeep of a historic house. Brigitte Bury Dervault wanted the house to reflect her own personal style, mingling family furniture with the work of designers who are friends or whom she admires. "I have the pleasure of being able to serve lunch on plates by the artist Sophie Calle or on an antique service that belonged to my grandmother. Having been fortunate enough to work for Baccarat, I have quite a collection of pretty glasses that I use on a daily basis in the kitchen and the garden, very casually." Most often, Brigitte Bury Dervault likes to entertain under an arbor, on the terrace, in the garden, or even in the park on fine summer days—often with twenty-five guests or more.

"I imagine the decorations like miniature stage sets, according to whatever inspires me. We often give buffet lunches, but always with a seating plan: out of the question for friends to congregate together at the same table! A lot of the pleasure in entertaining lies in setting up interactions between people who may enjoy each other's company." No rigid planning when it comes to menus. An accomplished cook, the hostess lets herself by guided by her instincts, depending on what's in season in the market. A typical menu might include blushing tomato tarts and aïoli with vegetables in every shade of green. The colors of the dishes inspire the choice of tablecloth, plates, and glasses. With this color palette in mind, Brigitte Bury Dervault then grabs her secateurs and heads out into the garden to cut the flowers and branches to add the final touches to her table settings—an *art de vivre* bursting with color!

FACING PAGE
Brigitte Bury Dervault and her husband, Maurice Dervault—secateurs in hand—after cutting roses in the gardens of their Provençal domain.

RIGHT
A shady avenue leads up to Le Domaine des Sources, a handsome eighteenth-century country house that stayed in a family from Apt for one hundred and fifty years before becoming the retreat of Brigitte Bury Dervault and Maurice Dervault.

ABOVE, LEFT, AND FACING PAGE
Poppy the dog exploring the gardens: laid out as so many small theater sets, they include the pool, fountains, pergolas, and hedges that are meticulously clipped by Maurice Dervault and his teams of gardeners.

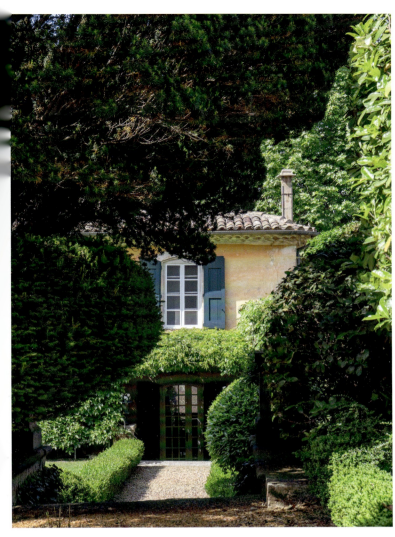

LEFT
An antique globe stands in the center of a pool, beneath the gaze of a nineteenth-century Chinese portrait bought from an antique dealer in Shanghai.

FACING PAGE
A spectacular chandelier with cardboard drops accented with Baccarat crystal pendants, created by the interior designer Jean Oddes.

BELOW
Soft, natural fabrics in one of the bedrooms.

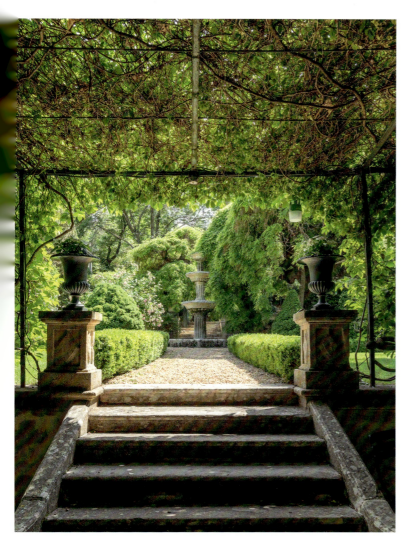

FACING PAGE, ABOVE, AND RIGHT
Under the pergola, Brigitte Bury Dervault likes to dress tables with cloths that echo the tones of the plasterwork of the façade. The early 1900s daybed and garden furniture lend this shady spot a timeless charm.

Provençale Tart with Tapenade

Ingredients (serves 4)

1 pack rectangular ready-rolled
 butter puff pastry
5 onions
4 tbsp olive oil, plus extra for the tapenade
 and for drizzling
Cherry tomatoes (yellow, red, orange)
1 zucchini
1 eggplant
Grated Parmesan
Basil leaves, to garnish
Salt and freshly ground black pepper

FOR THE TAPENADE

1 1/3 cups (9 oz./250 g) black olives, pitted
1 clove garlic
6 anchovy fillets in oil
2 tsp capers in vinegar

Method

Preheat the oven to 400°F (180°C/Gas Mark 6).

Line a rectangular tart pan with the pastry.

Slice the onions finely, then sauté them in a skillet with 4 tablespoons of olive oil, until they are very soft and cooked almost to a purée.

Spread the onion mixture over the pastry.

To make the tapenade, chop the olives and garlic. Drain the anchovy fillets, dry them on a paper towel, and chop finely. Drain the capers and put them in a blender with the olives and anchovies. Blend well, gradually adding olive oil to obtain a smooth, soft consistency.

Spread the tapenade over the onion mixture on the pastry.

Halve the cherry tomatoes, slice the zucchini and eggplant into thin rounds, and arrange them over the tapenade.

Drizzzle with olive oil and season lightly with salt and pepper. Sprinkle with grated Parmesan.

Bake in the oven for 25 minutes.

To serve, garnish with basil leaves.

Françoise Dumas

How to address royalty? Or write an invitation? Or work out a seating plan? No one knows the rules and codes of etiquette and protocol better than she does. As head of a public relations agency that specializes in event planning, Françoise Dumas describes herself—not entirely seriously—as "mistress of ceremonies." But, like all of us, sometimes she just feels the need to get away from it all.

She confesses like a naughty child: "Every school vacation—in other words, All Saints' Day in November, Christmas, Easter, and most of the summer—I go and hide away in my secret cabin." True, although in this case the hideaway is in the sought-after destination of Comporta, Portugal, where she has fallen under the spell of its endless beaches and unspoiled pine forests, ideal for long bike rides. Her refuge is surrounded by a walled garden, hidden away behind an oleander hedge. She bought a village house from a local farmer, and her great friend the interior designer Jacques Grange redesigned it throughout, remodeling the spaces, creating openings, and imbuing it with an irresistible charm. A delightful dollhouse of a building, it now boasts two bedrooms and a large living room, where Colombian baskets are mixed with ceramics by Bela Silva and chairs from Yves Saint Laurent and Pierre Bergé's château at Deauville. Pierre Passebon, another longtime accomplice, also offered some sound advice on the selection of the objects presented here. The only drawback was the lack of a proper dining room—because when she is there on vacation, relaxing into living *au naturel*, Françoise Dumas likes to entertain. So Jacques Grange built a cabin at the bottom of the garden where she could give lunches and dinners: "Never more than ten or twelve people—more than that and we won't all fit!"

Her basket under the arm, Françoise Dumas sets off to do her shopping and find treats with which to regale her guests: "For a successful party you need a pretty tablecloth, flowers from the garden, crockery from a flea market, and dishes made with local ingredients. Entertaining on vacation shouldn't be overly complicated—or, at least, it shouldn't seem that way." How does Françoise Dumas define the art of living? "Knowing how to savor the beauty all around you. What could give more pleasure than picking lemongrass from the garden to make a herbal tea? You have to go out and find beauty, go and discover the artisans in local villages, hunt down bargains at flea markets. The way to find happiness is to open your eyes."

FACING PAGE
A simple log cabin—although decorated with glazed plates from Caldas da Rainha—is the venue where the grande dame of the Paris social scene likes to entertain her nearest and dearest at her vacation home.

ABOVE, LEFT, AND FACING PAGE
Engulfed in greenery, the fisherman's cottage revisited by Françoise Dumas is a secret hideaway. The covered terrace makes a shady spot to enjoy breakfast or lunch with friends and family.

ABOVE
A table laid in the shade of the garden.

FACING PAGE
The guest table is laid out in a log cabin. Françoise Dumas maximizes the possibilities in order to accommodate different types of parties.

FACING PAGE, ABOVE, AND RIGHT
Plant themes and color palettes echo each other in the decorations and hand-crafted ceramics of the table settings.

Gratin of Baby Vegetables with Goat Cheese

Ingredients (serves 6)

¾ lb. (350 g) white part of leek
¾ lb. (350 g) baby turnips
¾ lb. (350 g) Chioggia beets
¾ lb. (350 g) purple beets
Scant ½ cup (100 ml) olive oil
Zest and juice of 1 lemon
Zest and juice of 1 orange
10 oz. (300 g) goat cheese (medium mature)
Salt and freshly ground black pepper

Method

Slice the leek into ½ in. (1 cm) rounds and boil in water with 2 teaspoons of salt for 3 minutes. Drain in a colander and set aside.

Wash the turnips and beets well to remove any soil. Slice very finely with a mandolin and place in a bowl.

Season with 2 teaspoons of salt, pepper, olive oil, lemon juice and zest, orange juice and zest, and marinate for 20 minutes.

Meanwhile preheat the oven to 425°F (200°C/Gas Mark 7).

Remove the vegetables from the marinade and put them in a small baking dish.

Place parchment paper over the vegetables, pressing down to make them adhere to the paper.

Cover and seal the baking dish very carefully with aluminum foil to prevent air from escaping and allow the vegetables to steam.

Bake in the oven for 30–40 minutes, or until the vegetables are just cooked.

Set the oven to broil. Remove the dish from the oven. Remove the aluminum foil and parchment paper.

Tear the goat cheese into small pieces and scatter with the leek over the vegetables. Return to the oven until golden on top.

Serve hot.

BELOW
Hand-painted shells act as place cards.

Green Apple Tart with Lemon Verbena Sugar

Ingredients (serves 6)

FOR THE LEMON VERBENA SUGAR
1 3/4 oz. (50 g) fresh lemon verbena leaves
1/3 cup (1 3/4 oz./50 g) confectioners' sugar

FOR THE SWEET SHORTCRUST PASTRY
1 1/3 sticks (5 1/4 oz./150 g) unsalted butter, at room temperature
1/2 cup (4 oz./110 g) white sugar
1 egg yolk
1/2 beaten egg
2 1/4 cups (10 oz./280 g) all-purpose flour
Dried beans (for baking blind)

FOR THE FILLING
5 Granny Smith apples
Juice of 2 lemons
1/2 cup (3 1/2 oz./100 g) sugar
2/3 stick (2 1/2 oz./75 g) butter

Method

The day before, dry the lemon verbena leaves in the oven overnight at 104°F (40°C).

The following day, put the dried verbena leaves in a blender and reduce them to a powder. Mix with the confectioners' sugar.

To make the shortcut pastry, beat the butter and sugar together until pale and smooth.

One at a time, beat in the egg yolk, beaten egg, and flour until they are well mixed, but without working the pastry too much.

Wrap in plastic wrap and allow to rest in the refrigerator for 1 hour.

Preheat the oven to 350°F (160°C/Gas Mark 4).

Using a rolling pin, roll out the pastry dough to a thickness of 1/8 in. (3 mm). Line a round tart pan with a removable base with the pastry. Trim the overhanging edges.

Cover the base of the pastry with parchment and dried beans. Bake in the oven for 20 minutes.

Remove the beans and bake for an additional 10–15 minutes, until the base is cooked through and golden.

Remove from the oven and allow to cool.

Preheat the oven to 400°F (180°C/Gas Mark 6).

To make the filling, peel the apples and cut them in slices around 1/8 in. (3 mm) thick. Put them in a bowl and cover them with water and lemon juice to prevent them from turning brown.

Drain the apple slices and pat them dry, then arrange them evenly over the bottom of the pre-cooked tart case, sprinkle with white sugar, and dot the top with butter.

Bake in the oven for 20–30 minutes, until the apple is cooked and the sugar and butter have melted. Allow to cool for at least 15 minutes before removing from the pan.

To serve, dredge with the lemon verbena sugar.

PAGES 126–127
The terrace overlooking the flowerbeds in the garden has a natural feel.

ABOVE
A guest room is lit by a pair of vintage glass-bead wall sconces under an artwork by José Canudo.

FACING PAGE
A club chair in natural fiber on a Berber rug, beneath the paired images of another artwork by José Canudo.

Nathalie Farman-Farma

With her passion for reading, Nathalie Farman-Farma designs fabrics that tell stories, in the way that a writer might pen an autobiographical novel. Her designs, which draw on her family roots as well as world cultures, are an expression of inner universes that are warm, welcoming, and serene.

She chose the name Décors Barbares for her line of fabrics in tribute to the Ballets Russes of Serge Diaghilev (1872–1929), who, after staging *Shéhérazade* at the Paris Opera, declared: "If Russians used to be viewed as barbarians, nowadays we view them as refined barbarians." As soon as you step through the door of Nathalie Farman-Farma's London home, your eye is caught by a host of different motifs, with Ikats reworked on living-room cushions and rugs from the Caucasus in dialogue with nineteenth-century furniture and elaborately crafted bibelots. Styles layer and overlap in a kaleidoscope of references. Are we plunged into a world of Proustian remembrances, or the hushed ambience of an Edith Wharton novel? Perhaps the romantic re-readings of the nineteenth century, in the manner of Madeleine Castaing? The atmosphere is evanescent, timeless.

It was while decorating her family home, where her two children Alexander and Rose grew up, that Nathalie Farman-Farma decided to launch her own collection: "I wanted it to be rooted in history and give the impression of antique textiles from somewhere else, but without too many identifiable references and with a veil of mystery." The interiors of her home are constantly evolving as her ideas change, and pieces may migrate from a bedroom to the living room on a whim.

The home also boasts an adjoining studio, which Nathalie Farman-Farma uses as both a design atelier and a showroom for displaying her collections of textiles and folk costumes. "It's also an ideal place for getting together with friends. My style of entertaining is very relaxed, so an artist's studio is the perfect setting. I keep a sort of open house. Friends come and go as they please. The key thing is the ambience. In my mind I see the event as a kind of experience in an enchanted space—or at least that's what I hope for, my secret aim. The flowers, music, and choice of tablecloths set the mood. For the buffet, I try to offer something for everyone, always with a vegetarian option. The dishes on the menu will dictate the plates and accessories that I choose for the evening. The art of living is something you learn with time, as the name suggests. It's about trusting your own tastes and imagination. The main thing is to relax and be ready to enjoy yourself as soon as the guests arrive!"

FACING PAGE
Nathalie Farman-Farma working on her fabric collections in the design studio adjoining her London home, which is also her showroom.

FACING PAGE AND PAGES 134-135
Vintage fabric samples, a gouache of a woman in Russian folk costume, and engravings of personal significance imbue a dreamlike interior with a nostalgic flavor.

BELOW
A tray of tempting Mediterranean-inspired appetizers.

Potato Gâteau

Ingredients (serves 6)

2 ½ lb. (1.2 kg) potatoes
Butter, for greasing
2 packs round ready-rolled butter puff pastry
1 egg yolk, beaten
2 generous tbsp crème fraîche
Salt and freshly ground black pepper

Method

Preheat the oven to 425°F (200°C/Gas Mark 7).

Peel the potatoes and slice them finely, as for a gratin. Pat them dry.

Grease a sheet of aluminum foil with butter. Place one of the puff pastry rounds on the foil. Top it with layers of potatoes, seasoning with salt and pepper as you go, and leaving a 1 in. (2 cm) border all round. Moisten the border with water.

Cover with the second puff pastry round, and with your fingers press the pastry edges together to seal them.

Baste the top with the beaten egg yolk.

Bake in the oven for 50 minutes.

Remove from the oven and make a hole in the center to add two generous spoonfuls of crème fraîche.

Return to the oven for an additional 10 minutes, protecting the top with aluminum foil if necessary.

PAGES 138–139
The table decorations evoke the sweetness of spring and childhood.

Fruit Crumble

Ingredients (serves 6)

Scant 1 cup (4 ½ oz./125 g) flour
½ cup (4 ½ oz./125 g) sugar
1 ⅓ cups (4 ½ oz./125 g) ground almonds
1 ½ sticks (6 oz./175 g) butter, well chilled
Fruits in season (here, apples and raspberries)
Demerara sugar to taste
Pinch salt

Method

Preheat the oven to 400°F (180°C/Gas Mark 6).

In a food processor, mix the flour, sugar, ground almonds, butter, and salt, to make a breadcrumb-like mixture.

Butter an oven dish.

Arrange the fruit (peeled and sliced as necessary) in the dish, add a little water and demerara sugar (depending on the moisture content and sweetness of the fruit), and cover with the crumble mixture.

Bake in the oven for around 30 minutes, until the fruit is bubbling and the crumble is golden.

BELOW
The dining room walls are hung with a vintage Braquenié fabric and decorated with framed vintage Russian embroideries.

FACING PAGE
Nathalie Farman-Farma chose the delicate, airy hue of the sky-blue paint on the sitting room walls to complement the riot of prints that dominate the space.

FACING PAGE AND ABOVE
Nathalie Farman-Farma has hung the walls of her bedroom with a Madeleine Castaing fabric, while the bedhead is covered with Dans la Forêt cotton fabric by Décors Barbares. Russian icons hang on the wall. Standing on the bedside tables are vintage silver-plated Argand lamps.

Laura Gonzalez

Famed for her skill in mixing graphics, prints, and colors, Laura Gonzalez has invented a style that scintillates—just as she herself does. It can be admired in the design of Cartier boutiques from Place Vendôme to Fifth Avenue, in the suites of the Saint James Paris hotel, and in her country showroom, a handsome house in the Vexin region of Normandy where she likes to entertain clients, coworkers, and friends for weekends that are both productive and pleasurable.

"I've always loved to entertain," says the Parisian interior designer. "While I tend instinctively to compartmentalize my professional and private life, I'm very happy mixing relatives with old friends, and since some of my clients have become close friends it actually feels quite open. What matters is that it should be convivial and fun, never stiff or starchy. As time passes, I find I enjoy giving lunches more and more. In the summer, it's at tables on the lawn; in the winter, in the warmth of the dining room." In order to showcase the furniture she designs and produces, and to invite those with an aesthetic eye to admire her creativity and potential clients to test the comfort of her seating, she has imagined a new type of space, where designer workspace meets family home.

In place of a traditional Normandy manoir or English country house, she likes to create interiors with a touch of surrealism, where chimney breasts become bear's heads or monkeys from a children's book. With her passion for high craftsmanship, she commissioned these two outsize animal ceramic bas-reliefs from the sculptor Laurent Dufour. Equally unexpectedly, you are barely through the door before you come upon brilliantly colorful Sicilian folk chairs in dialogue with a vintage chest of drawers adorned with colored shells. She is just as imaginative in her cooking. "I love to cook! I like to mix and match, in decorative styles and in flavors, whether traditional French, oriental, or Indian. I like to explore different cultures and bring the unexpected to my table, and not just in my choice of tablecloths!"

For Laura Gonzalez, *art de vivre* and *joie de vivre* go hand in hand, and have done ever since she started out in 2008. Star of the decorating revival, Laura Gonzalez breathes freshness and happiness into French classicism. At the age of 24 and still a student at Paris-Malaquais, she launched her own agency. The Bus Palladium decor launched her career. A number of successful restaurants followed, including Manko, La Lorraine and Lapérouse. Large-scale projects, such as the Cartier boutiques around the world and the renovation of the Saint James Paris hotel, confirmed her talent for festive, joyful, sparkling interiors. In her own image.

FACING PAGE
Laura Gonzalez in her country showroom, cuddling her labradoodle Paloma. The sofa on which she sits is one of her own designs, as is the coffee table with glazed ceramic top in the foreground.

ABOVE
Paco the golden retriever sets off for a walk in the gardens. Behind him rises the brick-and-render façade of the nineteenth-century house.

FACING PAGE
Looking through the enfilade of ground-floor rooms from the entrance doorway painted in trompe-l'œil faux marble.

ABOVE AND LEFT
A vintage commode covered in shells stands in the entrance hall. Arranged on coffee tables are ceramic frogs by Jean Roger and finds from flea markets.

FACING PAGE
In the living room, Laura Gonzalez commissioned the sculptor Laurent Dufour to make a bear bas-relief to decorate the chimney breast.

PAGES 152–153
Shelves of blue plates and glass and
the Antibes table designed by Laura Gonzalez,
with a top in hand-painted lava stone.

FACING PAGE, ABOVE, RIGHT, AND PAGES 156–157
Antique tableware, crystal, Murano glasses,
and silver candlesticks found in antique shops
and flea markets are arranged on a Rainbow table
with a multicolored raku ceramic marquetry top,
crafted by specialist Fabienne L'Hostis.

Red Lentil Dhal with Spinach and Coconut Milk

Ingredients (serves 6)

1 onion
1 clove garlic
1 tbsp organic coconut oil
1 tbsp grated fresh ginger
1 tbsp yellow curry paste
1 tsp turmeric
1 tsp ground cumin
1 tsp paprika
1 ½ cups (10 ½ oz./300 g) yellow lentils
1 ¼ cups (400 ml) coconut milk
1 cup (11 oz./300 g) tomato purée
1 ½ cups (9 oz./250 g) basmati rice
1 ½ cups (1 ¾ oz./50 g) baby spinach
Cinnamon
Salt and freshly ground black pepper

Method

Peel and finely chop the onion and the garlic.

In a frying pan, sauté the onion and garlic in the coconut oil with the ginger, yellow curry paste, turmeric, cumin, and paprika.

Rinse the lentils then add them to the pan.

Add the coconut milk and tomato purée, then cover and cook over a low heat for 30 minutes.

Meanwhile, cook the basmati rice.

Add the baby spinach to the lentil mixture, sprinkle with cinnamon, and cook for an additional 5 minutes.

Check the lentils are cooked and soft. Cook for an additional few minutes if necessary.

Adjust the seasoning and serve immediately with the rice.

• Tip from Laura •
Serve with fresh herbs, sliced bananas, cucumber raita and mint sauce.

Indian Coconut Custard with Passion Fruit

Ingredients (serves 6)

6 green cardamom pods
2 ½ cups (600 ml) coconut milk
1 cup (5 oz./150 g) demerara sugar
4 eggs
6 passion fruit

Method

Preheat the oven to 325°F (145°C/Gas Mark 3).

Open the cardamom pods, collect the little black seeds, and crush them.

Heat the coconut milk with the demerara sugar. When the sugar has melted, remove from the heat, add the cardamom seeds, and allow to infuse for 10 minutes.

Boil some water. Place your mold in a larger ovenproof dish and fill the dish with hot water to halfway up the mold.

Beat the eggs well and add the sweetened milk, stirring constantly. Pour the mixture into the mold.

Cook in the oven for 20 minutes. Remove the mold from the bain-marie.

Put the mold in the refrigerator for 2 hours. Slice the passion fruit in half and spoon the seeds over the custard.

FACING PAGE
The Pierre Frey wallpaper features an extravaganza of flowers in full bloom.

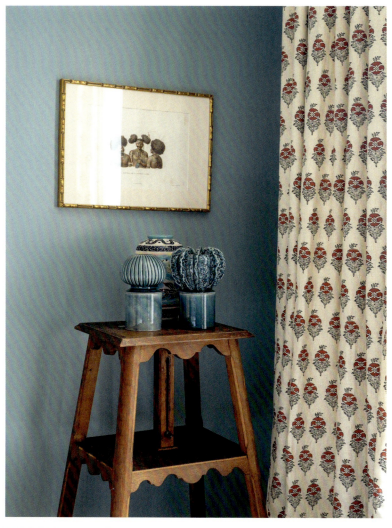
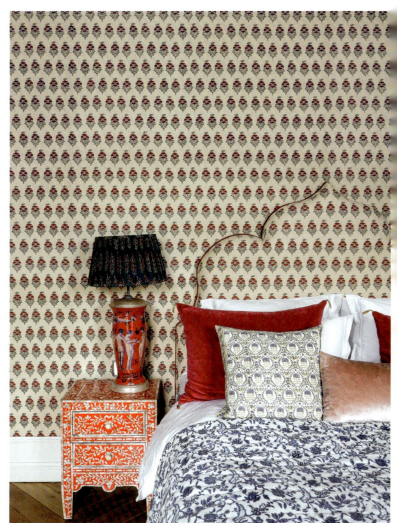

ABOVE
A set of ceramics designed by Laura Gonzalez displayed on a set of shelves and a bedroom featuring floral motifs.

LEFT
The handsome hand-painted clawfoot bathtub sits on a mosaic tile floor by Pierre Mesguich.

FACING PAGE
The Giraffe bedroom, with its Le Manach animal-motif wallpaper, features an Uzbek *suzani* throw and heaps of cushions in shimmering colors and designs.

Olympia and Ariadne Irving

With their mother, Carolina, sisters Olympia and Ariadne run the Carolina Irving & Daughters decorating line, which revisits period styles and designs in tableware, tablecloths, and candleholders in a vibrant color palettes. Raised in New York, they now live together in London.

They share a taste for walls in bold colors, prints, antique furniture, and handmade ceramics. In their house in northeast London, family heirlooms borrowed from their parents—eighteenth-century engravings, Swedish silver, and antique paintings—mingle with flea-market finds and salvaged pieces. The IKEA sofa in the living room is covered in Nino fabric, one of their mother's designs. Tables bought on Amazon are draped with colorful fabrics. On the mantelpiece, coral, Murano glass, and seashells are heaped together. Assembled instinctively, their interiors are full of imagination, charm, and wit. "One of the most important things our parents have taught us was not to be afraid. When it comes to decorating, you try things out, you see if they work, and that's it!" they laugh.

They work in the sunny conservatory, cluttered with prototypes of their ceramics, manufactured in Portugal. And they entertain there, too. "At weekends, we like to organize long lunches. Olympia cooks and I set the table," says Ariadne. "We each play our own part. We set out trays with condiments and vases overflowing with mixed bunches of flowers, we have a good playlist in the background, and in the evening, lots of candles. We entertain in different parts of the house, depending on the occasion and the number of guests. For small dinners, we like to use the conservatory. For larger ones, we eat in the dining room. Sometimes we have movie evenings in the living room and we eat on trays. Our house is like a kind of moveable feast."

The dining room is painted a deep apple green, Ariadne's bedroom is arsenic green, and Olympia's is soft pink. Unexpected splashes of zingy color explode everywhere. "For anyone else this house could be a nightmare. For us, it's an accumulation of memories. An interior isn't meant to please other people, it's a place designed for you. You don't have to bow to the latest trends—only if you like them."

FACING PAGE
Olympia and Ariadne Irving at one of the sash windows of their London house, with its typical yellow-brick façade.

BELOW
A collection of ceramic vases, dishes, and plates displayed on shelves against a back painted in colorful deckchair stripes.

RIGHT
In the conservatory, a wooden bench is strewn with brightly patterned cushions.

PAGES 168–169
The curtains are made from a tablecloth from the Carolina Irving & Daughters collection, while the dining chairs are covered with a Portuguese fabric. The painting on the wall belonged to Ariadne and Olympia's grandfather.

PAGES 172–173
The living room is filled with books and a kaleidoscope of patterns.

174–175
Dried botanical specimens decorate Olympia's bedroom, along with eighteenth-century paintings of gardens, and travel souvenirs.

Fresh Tomato and Garlic Pasta

Ingredients (serves 4)

9 oz. (250 g) fresh pasta
2 tbsp olive oil
2 cloves garlic, finely choppped
1 lb. 2 oz. (500 g) cherry tomatoes, halved
1 bunch basil, to garnish
Salt

Method

Cook the pasta in a big pan of salted water until al dente. Drain, add a little olive oil, and refrigerate to cool.

Meanwhile, mix the rest of the olive oil, the finely chopped garlic, and halved cherry tomatoes in a bowl. Season to taste with salt and refrigerate.

When the pasta is cold, tip the tomato mixture over it and mix gently. To serve, garnish with basil leaves.

Endive Salad with Roquefort and Walnuts

Ingredients (serves 4)

FOR THE SALAD
5 endives
$^2/_3$ cup (3 $^1/_2$ oz./100 g) coarsely chopped walnuts
Scant $^1/_2$ cup (1 $^3/_4$ oz./50 g) crumbled Roquefort
1 tsp finely chopped chives

FOR THE VINAIGRETTE
1 tsp mustard
2 tbsp white wine vinegar
3 tbsp olive oil
Salt and freshly ground black pepper

Method

Wash the endives, cut off the base, and separate the individual leaves. In a salad bowl, put the coarsely chopped walnuts, crumbled Roquefort, and finely chopped chives.

To make the vinaigrette, mix the mustard, vinegar, salt, and pepper. Add the oil and mix well.

Pour the vinaigrette over the walnuts, Roquefort, and chives and mix together. Arrange the endive leaves on a dish, spoon some of the Roquefort and walnut mixture into the hollow of each leaf, and serve.

Isabelle Moltzer

Isabelle Moltzer is a decorator, publisher of the dreamlike furniture created by her father Kim Moltzer (1938–2015), accomplished hostess, and cordon bleu chef, who also organizes highly successful dinners for an elite clientele in Paris. She likes to spend her weekends at the Château de Millemont.

Is it the classical layout of this eighteenth-century building, its beautiful ceramic-tiled dining room, or the long, shady driveways—perfect for long walks with her dog Thérèse—that bring Isabelle Moltzer to this home belonging to dear friends every weekend? One reason is certainly the need to escape the hectic pace of a busy Parisian life. For, not content with being a sought-after guest at dinner parties, she also enjoys organizing them for others, and has a knack for setting a deceptively formal table on a denim tablecloth strewn with wacky knick-knacks and witty glassware.

For Isabelle Moltzer, this quirky approach to entertaining has become a business in its own right. Yet it all started almost by chance. "About ten years ago, my friend Pierre Sauvage, who liked the way I entertained, asked me to organize a private dinner for a brand of whisky; it would never have occurred to me! I said I would, and after that it just carried on." From private parties to product launches and fine dinners for auction houses, she organizes one chic event after another, taking care of everything, from the table decorations to the dishes she serves: "But I don't claim to be a chef or a caterer, I just do good home cooking, dishes that are full of flavor, uncomplicated, and unpretentious." This also describes her elegantly laid-back tables, with a preference for denim tablecloths over immaculately starched affairs. For silverware, crockery, and glasses, she delves deep into her personal collections. "I already had quite a few things, but now I just buy and buy—it's compulsive! I love to mix things up, to create something slightly unexpected." With her china and silverware, pots and pans, and her ingredients, all unloaded from her little van, she gets down to the cooking: "I always cook on site: reheated risotto is inedible!"

She also sometimes works at the Château de Millemont, some of whose buildings date back to Francis I of France, the most recent dating from 1710. She arrives with her piles of plates, which she likes to mix with local finds from the cupboards. "Sometimes I think I should have been a jewelry designer—another of my passions. It's less heavy to lug around! Who knows, maybe I should get into it."

FACING PAGE
Isabelle Moltzer and her dog Thérèse on a walk down one of the avenues lined with clipped hedges in the château grounds.

PAGES 178–179
The Château de Millemont, an hour from Paris.

ABOVE
An early eighteenth-century family portrait hangs against a nineteenth-century sprigged fabric.

FACING PAGE
The neoclassical architecture of an interior courtyard, redolent of the spirit of the Enlightenment.

PAGES 182–183, FACING PAGE, RIGHT, AND BELOW
In the dining room, formerly the *rotisserie* of the château kitchens, the denim tablecloth echoes the blues of the ceramic wall tiles. The Italian plates with their borders of dancers and figures on horseback were a find from the Place Saint-Sulpice flea market in Paris.

Sealed Scallops

Ingredients (serves 4)

½ stick (2 oz./55 g) unsalted butter
1 tbsp grated fresh ginger
2 tbsp chopped cilantro
Juice of 1 lime
4 scallops (minus coral) and 4 whole shells (concave and flat sides)
1 pack rectangular ready-rolled butter puff pastry
Salt and freshly ground black pepper

Method

Preheat the oven to 400°F (180°C/Gas Mark 6).

Melt the butter. Add the ginger and cilantro, salt and pepper, and lime juice.

Place a scallop in each of the concave shells, then top with 2 tablespoons of the ginger and cilantro mixture.

Cut 4 strips of pastry 2 in. (5 cm) wide.

Place the flat scallop shells over the concave shells and seal the shells all round with the strips of puff pastry.

Bake for 10 minutes.

Kim's Argentinian *Hachis Parmentier* (Shepherd's Pie)

Ingredients (serves 8)

FOR THE MEAT LAYER
5 eggs
1 onion, chopped
2 shallots
1 clove garlic
Sweet paprika
Thyme
Oregano
½ can peeled tomatoes
1 lb. 2 oz. (500 g) medium-ground beef, moist and lightly veined with fat
1 lb. 2 oz. (500 g) medium-ground lamb, half neck, half shoulder
Coarsely chopped black olives
Currants
2 glasses Noilly Prat (French Vermouth)
Beef stock (Ariaké by Robuchon, or homemade)
Salt and freshly ground black pepper

FOR THE MASHED POTATO
3 ¼ lb. (1.5 kg) floury potatoes
2 tbsp butter
Generous cup (300 ml) milk
2 tbsp crème fraîche
Nutmeg

Method

Hard-boil the eggs, then allow to cool.

To make the meat layer, sauté the chopped onion, shallots, and garlic in a casserole dish, stirring frequently until well browned. Add the paprika, thyme, oregano, tomatoes, salt, and pepper, and cook for an additional 5–10 minutes.

Add the ground meats, coarsely chopped black olives, currants, and Noilly Prat. Moisten with the beef stock. Simmer for 35–40 minutes.

Meanwhile, make the mashed potato: peel and slice the potatoes and cook them in a large pan of salted water. Drain.

In a bowl, mash the potatoes, gradually adding the butter, milk, cream, and nutmeg.

Preheat the oven to 425°F (200°C/Gas Mark 7).

Put the meat mixture in a gratin dish. Peel the hard-boiled eggs, slice them in rounds, and arrange them on top of the meat mixture. Cover with the mashed potato and decorate the top with a fork.

Bake in the oven for 20 minutes, until the mashed potato is golden brown.

Ultra-Creamy Chocolate Cream

Ingredients
(makes 8 medium-sized ramekins)

9 oz. (250 g) 55 % dark chocolate
3 cups (750 ml) heavy cream

Method

Break the chocolate into small pieces. In a saucepan, bring the cream to simmering point over a medium heat.

Remove from the heat, add the chocolate, and whisk until melted. Once the chocolate has melted, put the pan back over a medium heat and bring the mixture back to simmering point, whisking frequently. Once the mixture has started to simmer, continue whisking for an additional 2 minutes.

Remove from the heat and pour into eight ramekins. Leave in a cool place to set for at least half a day.

Almond and Honey Tart

Ingredients (serves 6)

2/3 stick (2 1/2 oz./75 g) unsalted butter
1/3 cup (2 1/2 oz./75 g) demerara sugar
1 tbsp honey
1 tbsp crème fraîche
1/2 cups (4 1/2 oz./125 g) flaked almonds
Scant 1/2 cup (2 oz./60 g) pine nuts
1 pack round ready-rolled sweet shortcrust pastry

Method

Preheat the oven to 400°F (180°C/Gas Mark 6). In a saucepan, melt the butter, then add, one by one, the sugar, honey, and crème fraîche. When the mixture starts to froth, add the almonds and pine nuts.

Spread the pastry on parchment paper and place on an oven shelf. Spread the almond and pine nut mixture on top, leaving a 3/4 in. (2 cm) border all round. Bake in the oven for 8–10 minutes.

RIGHT
A little theater was set up in the château orangery for the TF1 television series *Sam*, created by Claire Lemaréchal.

ABOVE
Enfilade with bookshelves on the piano nobile.

FACING PAGE
The main staircase in eighteenth-century neoclassical style.

Pascale Mussard

For the past decade, Pascale Mussard has presided over the Villa Noailles—the modernist icon built in the hills above Hyères by Robert Mallet-Stevens (1886–1945) in 1923—and is a beacon of light for young designers in the fields of fashion, design, and decoration.

Her style exudes a restrained elegance, enlivened by splashes of bold color and striking accessories. And while at first she may seem reserved—due to her perfect manners—when you draw her into a subject close to her heart, such as the arts, Pascale Mussard immediately reveals her true warmth, vibrancy, and attentiveness, always ready to embark on new ventures that are off the beaten track. A sixth-generation descendant of Thierry Hermès, she—along with her cousin Pierre-Alexis Dumas—was artistic director of the famous luxury house that started out as a saddlery. She then launched the company Petit h, pioneering the recycling of leather offcuts, and now looks after a stable of a different kind. As director of the Villa Noailles, she focuses her attention on fostering the talents of young artists in the applied arts, through the International Festival of Fashion, Photography and Accessories and the Design Parade: "These events are launch pads for discovering new generations of creatives and different ways of looking at the world. It's very exciting!"

At her home in Brussels, too, Pascale Mussard likes to surround herself with unusual and creative objects, such as a Tree Table by Charles Kaisin with chestnut-wood chairs by Christian Astuguevieille. Birds by the artist Julio Villani perch on a balustrade. Not to mention the Petit h swing, crafted out of a miscellany of horse accessories. It's a world of its own, quirky and cultured, an exhilarating mix of styles, provenances, and periods: "Objects have arrived by serendipity, really, through people I've met, discoveries I've made, and places I've visited. I'm surrounded by a lot of things, but every one of them has its natural place here." The result is an eclectic clutter of a highly artistic kind.

Pascale Mussard lives in an art nouveau studio designed by Ernest Blerot (1870–1957) for the painter and sculptor Louise De Hem (1866–1922). A balcony with a wrought-iron balustrade featuring plant motifs and friezes of ceramic tiles embellish the façade. The building is not lacking in style. With her passion for the arts, Pascale Mussard set about transforming part of it into an artist's residence, so that she can invite writers, musicians, and ceramists—having installed a kiln—into her enchanted world. "The house looks out over a garden that's a haven of peace and an aid to concentration." And to daydreaming, too.

FACING PAGE
Pascale Mussard hangs a garland from an arrangement of branches in her Brussels studio.

PAGES 196–197
A large table designed by Charles Kaisin, chairs, armchairs and temple by Christian Astuguevieille.

ABOVE AND FACING PAGE
Attelage stainless-steel silverware by Hermès, Apollo crystal glass by Saint-Louis, antique ceramics, salt and pepper grinders by Ettore Sottsass for Alessi, and children's toys combine to create a table setting filled with a joyous sense of fun.

Veal Loaf, Carrots, Heritage Vegetables, and Potatoes with Rosemary

Ingredients (serves 6)

FOR THE BÉCHAMEL SAUCE
½ stick (2 oz./55 g) butter
⅓ cup (1 ¾ oz./50 g) flour
2 ½ cups (600 ml) milk

FOR THE VEAL LOAF
1 lb. 2 oz. (500 g) veal scallop, cooked in advance, sliced, and cut in small pieces
14 oz. (400 g) cooked ham, cut in cubes
3 eggs, beaten
1 small onion, finely chopped
1 stick celery, finely chopped
2 cloves garlic, finely chopped
1 cup (2 oz./60 g) fresh breadcrumbs
1 tbsp tomato concentrate
Juice of 1 lemon
1 bunch tarragon, washed, leaves only
1 tsp paprika
1 tsp nutmeg
Thyme
Bay leaf
Butter, for the mold
Salt and freshly ground black pepper

FOR THE CARROTS
1 bunch carrots
A few baby onions, chopped.
2 tbsp (1 oz./28 g) butter

FOR THE HERITAGE VEGETABLES
(according to the produce in season)
3–4 parsnips
5–6 Jerusalem artichokes
3–4 rutabagas
2 turnips
3–4 carrots, if possible of different colors
1 lemon, sliced
Knob of butter
4 tbsp olive oil
¼ cup (3 ½ oz./100 g) honey
Cumin
1 sprig rosemary
Salt and freshly ground black pepper

FOR THE POTATOES WITH ROSEMARY
1 lb. 2 oz. (500 g) baby potatoes
Knob of butter
1 sprig rosemary
Salt

Method

Preheat the oven to 400°F (180°C/Gas Mark 6).

To make the béchamel sauce, melt the butter in a saucepan, add the flour, and stir with a wooden spoon without allowing the mixture to color. Gradually add the milk, stirring constantly, until the sauce thickens.

To make the veal loaf, add the chopped veal, ham, and the rest of the ingredients to the béchamel sauce and mix together. Tip into a lightly buttered, high-sided mold.

Bake in the oven for around 1 hour. The veal loaf may be eaten hot or cold.

Meanwhile, boil the carrots in water until cooked. Brown the chopped baby onions in butter. When the carrots are cooked, drain and mix with the onions.

For the heritage vegetables, peel, clean, and chop the vegetables, then either steam them with the lemon or boil them in salted water.

In a large skillet, melt a knob of butter with the olive oil and honey. Brown the vegetables in this, adding the cumin, salt and pepper, and a little rosemary at the end of cooking.

For the potatoes with rosemary, peel and slice the potatoes, boil them until cooked, then brown them in a skillet with chopped rosemary, butter, and sea salt.

Serve the carrots, heritage vegetables, and potatoes with the veal loaf.

PAGES 202–203
The living room, with its sofa covered with an original painted-canvas motif.

FACING PAGE
A woven-jute wall tapestry by Alexander Calder hangs beside the faceted metal fireplace by Fabian von Spreckelsen.

ABOVE AND RIGHT
An eclectic mix of engravings, constructivist figurines, folk art, and a Renaissance portrait.

Franz Potisek

The interior designer Franz Potisek excels in the art of galvanizing nineteenth-century Romanticism with touches of 1960s pop art. His apartment in the Nouvelle Athènes quarter of Paris takes neoclassicism and gives it a vibrant, zingy, imaginative twist, full of pizzaz.

The apartment is a stone's throw from the Grands Boulevards, a few steps from the Grand Rex cinema, and a block or two from the Drouot auction house, his favored haunt. His interiors undergo frequent transformations, according to his latest finds and passing fancies: "I change the furniture regularly; recently I designed a Napoleon III-style sofa for the living room." He also likes to design objects, furniture, and fabrics.

"I have masses of paintings in my closets. In the living room I've put statues mostly, in the nineteenth-century way." His passion for the 1880s goes back to childhood memories of a beautiful family home where several generations lived happily together. "Some of my aunts would make sure the fires were made up in the guest bedrooms, while others would bake cakes. For me, it was a house of happiness!" The tenth child in a large family, this self-taught collector has been amassing antiques since he was twelve, his first acquisition being an Empire mahogany bureau. Although he readily admits to his love of classicism, there is no danger of Franz Potisek resorting to tiresome historical pastiches. His mixtures of bold colors and scintillating patterns always have a touch of quirkiness. The bedroom walls are strewn with roses in a print that could hardly be more 1950s in style, while a different motif twinkles in the hallway.

This love of vintage style extends to his entertaining. Franz Potisek treats his guests to prawn cocktails, Baked Alaska, and other distinctly démodé delights. "I love to cook dishes that my mother and grandmother used to make for me. A lot of the pleasure of entertaining lies in watching your friends' eyes shine as you bring in the dishes." Juggling between different dinner services and choosing his tablecloths to match the season, he likes to add color to his table settings with masses of unusual objects such as opaline glass. "I entertain a lot, often with four to six people—eight means I have to go down to the cellar to get the table extensions, so I avoid it! I enjoy impromptu dinners most of all. I find them more relaxed, people are really pleased to see each other, there's a nice dynamic. With something formal, planned months in advance, it's not always like that." For Franz Potisek, it's the ambience that matters, even more than the objects, the food, or the flowers. "A successful dinner is an opportunity to express your *joie de vivre*."

FACING PAGE
Franz Potisek prepares to mix a stiff drink amid the 1960s-style charm of the kitchen in his apartment near the Grands Boulevards in Paris.

BELOW
Napkins embroidered with the host's initials.

FACING PAGE
A neoclassical bust presides over the dining room.

RIGHT
Franz Potisek brightens his table composition with a collection of little opaline vases, while a Gothic Revival chandelier adds a dramatic note.

FACING PAGE
Hyacinths and daffodils planted in silver tumblers add a breath of springtime to the table.

RIGHT
Bronze medallions and a neo-Renaissance *verre églomisé* chair accentuate the nineteenth-century character of the space.

Shrimp Cocktail

Ingredients (serves 4)

FOR THE VERRINE
16 good-sized shrimp
A few lettuce leaves
2 avocados
A few cherry tomatoes
1 grapefruit

FOR THE LIGHT COCKTAIL SAUCE
2 pots plain yogurt
2 tsp strong Dijon mustard
4 tbsp ketchup
1 tsp Worcestershire sauce
1 tbsp cognac
Salt and freshly ground black pepper

Method

To make the verrines, peel eight of the shrimp completely and slice them. Peel the remaining eight and leave their heads on.

Shred the lettuce leaves. Peel and slice the avocados. Halve the cherry tomatoes. Slice the peel and pith off the grapefruit and divide into supremes, slicing the flesh of each segment away from the membrane and removing any seeds.

Assemble each verrine in a cocktail glass, starting with the shredded lettuce, then the supremes of grapefruit, avocado, and chopped shrimp. Finish with the shrimp with their heads on and scatter with the tomato halves.

To make the sauce, mix together the yogurt and mustard, and season with salt and pepper. Taste and adjust the seasoning if necessary. Add the other ingredients and mix well.

Spoon over the verrines and serve chilled.

Shoulder of Lamb *à la Provençale*

Ingredients (serves 4)

1 lb. 5 oz. (600 g) firm potatoes
1 lb. 2 oz. (500 g) cherry tomatoes
1 bulb pink garlic
Olive oil
Thyme
1 good-quality shoulder of lamb
Rosemary
Neutral oil (sunflower, grapeseed, or groundnut), for sautéing
Salt and freshly ground black pepper

Method

Preheat the oven to 400°F (180°C/Gas Mark 6). Peel the potatoes and chop them into ½ in. (1.5 cm) cubes. Halve the cherry tomatoes.

On a baking tray, arrange the cherry tomatoes, without overlapping, drizzle with olive oil, season with salt and pepper, and sprinkle with thyme.

Bake in the oven for around 40 minutes, until the tomatoes start to shrivel a little without burning. Remove from the oven and keep warm.

Raise the oven temperature to 475°F (220°C/Gas Mark 9).

In an oven dish, place the shoulder of lamb on a bed of rosemary, baste it with olive oil, season it with salt and pepper, and roast in the oven for 15–20 minutes according to weight.

At the same time, put the unpeeled garlic cloves in a small baking dish, drizzle with olive oil, and roast for 15 minutes.

Remove the lamb from the oven and wrap it in two layers of aluminum foil. Keep warm for 15 minutes.

In a skillet, sauté the potatoes in neutral oil.

Arrange the potatoes in a serving dish, cover with the tomatoes and garlic cloves, and top with the shoulder of lamb.

Serve hot.

Baked Alaska

Ingredients (serves 4)

FOR THE RUM AND RAISIN ICE CREAM
Scant ½ cup (100 ml) rum (approx) + 1 tbsp
¾ cup (4 ½ oz./125 g) raisins
2 cups (500 ml) whole milk
1 vanilla pod
5 egg yolks
¾ cup (3 ½ oz./100 g) superfine sugar
Scant 1 cup (200 ml) crème fraîche

FOR THE BAKED ALASKA
Genoise cake
Italian meringue
Rum syrup
Flaked almonds

FOR THE FLAMBÉ
½ cup (150 ml) rum
3 ¼ tbsp (1 ½ oz./40 g) sugar

Method

To make the rum and raisin ice cream, tip the raisins into a saucepan with the rum and heat over a medium heat until the liquid is absorbed, around 10 minutes.

Pour the milk into another saucepan, with the vanilla pod, split open to release the seeds, and heat over a low heat without bringing to a boil.

In a bowl, beat the egg yolks with the sugar, incorporating a little of the hot milk and vanilla, then add this to the remaining milk in the saucepan. Stir constantly until the mixture thickens, then remove immediately from the heat.

When the mixture is at room temperature, put it in the refrigerator, preferably overnight, together with the rum-soaked raisins.

The following day, remove the vanilla pod and whisk the crème fraîche into the vanilla mixture, then pour into an ice-cream maker. Add a tablespoon of rum and the raisins. Refrigerate for several hours before serving.

To make the Baked Alaska, lay a ¾ in. (2 cm) layer of Genoise cake in the bottom of an oblong oven dish and soak it with rum syrup. Cover with around 2 in. (5 cm) of rum and raisin ice cream. Top with ¾ in. (2 cm) of Italian meringue, and decorate with a fork. Refrigerate for a few hours.

Preheat the oven at grill setting.

Meanwhile, put the rum and sugar in a saucepan and bring them to the boil.

To serve, sprinkle the Baked Alaska with flaked almonds and put under a hot grill to brown.

Remove the Baked Alaska from the oven and flambé immediately with the rum and sugar mixture in front of your guests.

PAGES 218–219
The living room, with its glowing colors and painted paneling enhanced with sculptures.

FACING PAGE AND RIGHT, TOP AND BOTTOM
Franz Potisek designed the 1950s-style floral motif in his bedroom, produced by Tissus Choisis par Casa Lopez.

ABOVE AND FACING PAGE
To breathe new life into the neoclassical décor of his apartment, Franz Potisek papered his entrance hall with a graphic motif on a pink background, produced by Tissus Choisis par Casa Lopez.

Rebecca de Ravenel

A jewelry designer who also designs bags and tableware, Rebecca de Ravenel lives and works by the sea. It's from a seaside destination with a peaceful charm that she imagines and develops her collections, combining charm and sophistication, casual chic and elegance—just like her.

It was a chance encounter that gave Rebecca de Ravenel the idea of launching her line. She was in a restaurant, wearing a pair of earrings she had made, when a man approached her to say he would like to give similar earrings to his wife. That was the catalyst. Since then, she has been selling her oversized, boldly colored designs on her website and in major US department stores. The idea of using silk cord for jewelry came to her when she was working for Oscar de la Renta, and she wanted jewelry that was as easy to wear for day as for night.

Rebecca de Ravenel grew up in the Bahamas until the age of seven, before moving to Paris for her education. She began her professional career in New York, initially working in public relations for houses such as Gucci and Tory Burch, before graduating from Parsons School of Design in New York and devoting herself to design. Back in the Bahamas for a while, she started working in interior design. Now based on a beach on the Atlantic Ocean, she lives in a house that is flooded with light and dominated by white accentuated with touches of blue, from the azulejo tabletop in her office to the ultramarine fish and wave motifs on her tableware, and the sky blue of the banquettes and cushions in the living room.

"My homes are always filled with life, books, objects, flowers, and dogs. It always feels like I've been there forever, even though I move house a lot," she explains. "Every time I move, I mix and match the things I've collected and been given over the years. My home is full of imperfections, layers, and personal stories." A smattering of carefully chosen antiques and big Venetian mirrors mixed with summery rattan furniture define an ambience that is as relaxed as it is elegant. It is in this romantic setting that she likes to entertain her friends. "Entertaining demands a minimum of care. Even if you entertain in the kitchen, people appreciate it if you make a little effort with your presentation. It shows them that you care, that you value their presence." Her secret for a successful evening? "Dishes that are simple but delicious, good conversation, and a happy atmosphere. I always take it as a great compliment when people linger late into the night."

FACING PAGE
Rebecca de Ravenel in her living room, presided over by an imposing Empire-style console table transformed into a decorative bar.

LEFT
The geometric lines of the living room sofa are echoed by the design of the banquette seating facing it. The room's central feature is the coffee table with its trompe l'œil painted top in imitation of a panther pelt.

ABOVE
The desk top covered with azulejo tiles, and the hostess's collection of straw hats and bags.

FACING PAGE
Where the fireplace once stood is now banquette seating.

Lemon Garlic Shrimp

Ingredients (serves 4)

1 tbsp butter or extra-virgin olive oil
1 lb. (450 g) medium shrimp, peeled and deveined
2 lemons, sliced but not peeled
3 cloves garlic, finely chopped
1 tsp crushed red pepper flakes
Salt
Juice of 1 lemon
2 tbsp water or white wine
Freshly chopped parsley, to garnish

Method

In a large skillet, melt 1 tablespoon of butter or olive oil over a medium heat. Add the shrimp, lemon slices, garlic, and crushed red pepper flakes, and season with salt.

Cook, stirring occasionally, until the shrimp are pink and opaque, about 3 minutes each side.

Remove from the heat, add the lemon juice and water or white wine, and season with salt.

To serve, sprinkle with parsley.

FACING PAGE
Posies of yellow irises add a warm, sunny note to the table.

BELOW
Woven baskets and small bowls hold shells and visiting cards.

FACING PAGE
An imposing mirror with a *verre églomisé* frame, set against a wall paneled with distressed mirror glass.

FACING PAGE AND ABOVE
In the main bedroom, a small English nineteenth-century desk embellished with faux bamboo is given a modern twist with a Zig Zag chair by the Dutch designer Gerrit Thomas Rietveld.

Remy Renzullo

Exuberantly bohemian in an open shirt and Venetian slippers, the American decorator Remy Renzullo evokes the tempestuous elegance of a Lord Byron (1788–1824), the epitome of British Romanticism.

He draws his inspiration from the pages of epic novels: "I read constantly—I prefer books to films, as they free my mind to imagine the settings of the places I'm reading about," he explains. "That being said, a lot of my documentation comes from my collection of auction catalogs." Raised in rural Connecticut, Remy credits his vocation to his mother, herself a decorator. His childhood home was a treasure store of furniture found in bric-à-brac shops–birds' nests, taxidermy, and old fabric remnants. It has left him with an enduring love of chiaroscuro décors and dreamy, nostalgic interiors.

Drawn to working in London, since he has as many English clients as American, he lives in a two-story apartment of undeniable charm at the top of a house in Islington. "I try to live simply and without too much stress—and the same is true of the interiors I design," he says. "I don't like things that are too strict or formal. My home is filled with seventeenth-, eighteenth-, and nineteenth-century antiques, but the way I live is modern, comfortable, and relaxed."

He enjoys entertaining in his apartment: "Sometimes just one guest, sometimes a large group. I always make simple dishes; I don't like food that is precious or complicated. Nothing could be more delicious than a roast chicken or a risotto. And I always make sure to have plenty of wine—I love it when people linger on for hours after dinner. If there are several of us, we play card games and sometimes we even dance. The most important thing is to be relaxed yourself, because the guests will follow the example of their host."

Remy Renzullo dresses his table with embroidered linen or damask tablecloths. "I'm particularly fond of pink damask. The best damasks were made in Ireland in the nineteenth century. My great-grandmother, who was a wonderful hostess, had dozens of sets of household linen made with magnificent motifs. I'm lucky that my mother inherited some of them, and we use them." His other passions include eighteenth- and nineteenth-century glass and ceramics: "I have a set of English Imari plates from 1840, which are very eye-catching! I'm constantly buying new sets of plates and running out of room to store them. As the dishes I serve are always simple, I make sure that my table is beautiful and interesting to look at." A diversionary tactic, maybe, but a successful one!

FACING PAGE
Sitting at his desk on a Regency chair, Remy Renzullo notes down the ideas, moods, and daydreams that will inspire the atmosphere of his current architectural projects.

FACING PAGE
The living room, with a bookcase that used to belong to Min Hogg.

BELOW AND PAGE 241
The tables are lit by candles and set with an antique Chinese porcelain service.

PAGE 240
A Barbotine-ware plate representing a sole.

Roast Chicken, a Very Old Family Recipe from Kentucky

Ingredients (serves 6)

FOR THE CHICKEN
1 organic chicken (around 5 ½ lb./2.5 kg)
½ lemon
Thyme sprigs
Rosemary sprigs
2 sticks (8 oz./220 g) butter
3 ¾ cups (950 ml) chicken stock (approx.)
Salt and freshly ground black pepper

FOR THE MASHED POTATOES
8 Yukon Gold potatoes
1 stick (4 oz./110 g) butter, sliced
½ cup (120 ml) heavy cream
Salt and freshly ground black pepper

FOR THE GRAVY
2 tbsp Wondra quick-mixing flour
⅓ cup (80 ml) cognac
¼ cup (60 ml) chicken stock
1 tsp Better Than Bouillon concentrated stock (optional)

Method

Preheat the oven to 400°F (180°C/Gas Mark 6).

Prepare the chicken. Put the half lemon and several sprigs of thyme and rosemary in the chest cavity of the chicken. Slide a knob of butter and 2 sprigs of thyme and rosemary under the skin on each side of the breast. Tie the legs together with cooking twine.

Place the chicken in a large enameled roasting pan, with a few small pieces of butter underneath. Pour ⅓ cup (80 ml) chicken stock over the chicken and in the pan.

Melt 3 tablespoons (1 ½ oz./45 g) butter and brush this over the chicken skin. Sprinkle with salt and pepper.

Roast in the oven for 15 minutes.

After 15 minutes, baste the chicken with the melted butter in the bottom of the pan, and if needed pour an additional ⅓ cup (80 ml) of chicken stock over the chicken.

Roast for around 90 minutes, basting every 15–20 minutes, until the skin is golden brown but not crispy.

Raise the oven temperature to 475°F (220°C/Gas Mark 9), baste one last time, and roast for an additional 15 minutes.

To check if the chicken is fully cooked, pierce the skin between the leg and the body: if the juices run clear, the chicken is cooked.

Transfer the chicken to a platter, keeping all the juices in the roasting pan, and tent with aluminum foil until serving.

While the chicken is cooking, make the mashed potatoes. Peel the potatoes and cut them in quarters. Put them in a saucepan and cover with cold water. Add a pinch of salt and bring to the boil.

Boil uncovered for around 10 minutes, until the potatoes feel soft when pricked with a fork. Drain the potatoes and put them back in the saucepan. Add half the butter and half the cream and mix using a potato masher. Continue to mash while adding the remaining butter and cream. The consistency should be smooth, but not as smooth as a purée. Season with salt and pepper.

To make the gravy, skim off half or more of the fat in the roasting pan and place the pan over the largest burner on the stovetop. Heat through on a medium-high heat.

When it starts to bubble, mix in the gravy flour and stir for 1 minute. Slowly add the cognac and stir with a large slotted spoon to deglaze the bottom of the pan.
Add the chicken stock, ¼ cup (60 ml) or so at a time, stirring constantly.

Once the gravy is the desired thickness and bubbling hot, reduce the heat to a slow simmer.

Carve the chicken quickly and serve immediately with lots of gravy.

• *Tip from Remy* •

Adjust the amount of chicken stock according to personal preference. For added flavor, add 1 teaspoon of Better Than Bouillon concentrated chicken stock and mix in.

Vanilla Ice Cream and Hot Fudge Sauce

Ingredients (serves 4)

FOR THE VANILLA ICE CREAM
1 cup (250 ml) crème fraîche
1 cup (250 ml) whole milk
¾ cup (3 ½ oz./100 g) superfine sugar
2 tbsp vanilla extract
Pinch salt

FOR THE SAUCE
2 oz. (55 g) unsweetened baking chocolate
1 tbsp butter
⅓ cup (80 ml) boiling water
1 cup (7 oz./200 g) sugar
2 tbsp corn syrup (or similar)
1 tsp vanilla extract

Method

To make the ice cream, mix all the ingredients together and put in an ice-cream maker for around 20 minutes (according to the model), or longer for a firmer consistency.

To make the sauce, melt the chocolate with the butter in a bain-marie on the stovetop, taking care not to let them burn.

Stir until well blended, then add the boiling water and stir well again. Add the sugar and corn syrup. Bring to the boil without stirring. Cover with a lid and boil for 3 minutes.

Remove the lid, reduce the heat and cook for an additional 2 minutes, still without stirring. Just before serving, stir in the vanilla extract.

Serve the ice cream in individual bowls and pour over a liberal amount of sauce.

PAGES 246–247
Above the living room fireplace, flanked by a pair of ceramic urns, hangs a George III mirror by John Booker, bought from the Dublin antique dealer Rory Rogers.

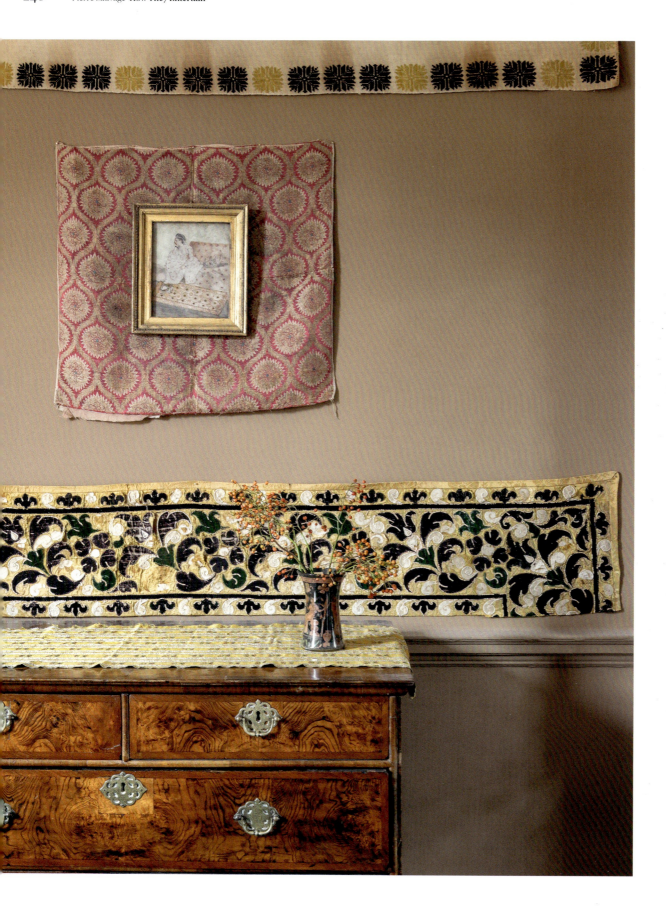

ABOVE
Pinned on the walls are samples of antique embroideries and silks.

FACING PAGE
In Remy Renzullo's bedroom, a vintage quilt is thrown over a nineteenth-century brass and iron bed.

Caroline Sarkozy

She loves the interplay between different textures, the vibrancy of colors, and interiors that exude comfort. Through her CSLB agency, Caroline Sarkozy designs homes in her own image: warm, welcoming, full of life—as may be seen in her Paris apartment on the banks of the Seine.

After graduating from the Parsons School of Design in New York, she learned the ropes with the iconic designer Andrée Putman, who passed on her love of taut lines and clean shapes, as well as her instinct for beautiful objects. "I can appreciate things with very different provenances and a wide variety of styles, but they all share one constant: I'm receptive to really good design," she says. "Above all else, I like an object to have its own presence, to exist in its own right." On her living room wall is a fabric triptych by the Malagasy artist Joël Andrianomearisoa; the spectacular floor lamp is by Studio Wieki Somers; in the bedroom, a straw marquetry chest of drawers is her own design. Her home is furnished with creations she has acquired over the years, through people she has met and her own changing tastes: "I bought the Hubert Le Gall coffee table for my first apartment over twenty years ago, and I've never grown tired of it." Mixing works by established designers with pieces by up-and-coming talents is the hallmark of Caroline Sarkozy's cultivated style.

  "I like to entertain at home, mixing old friends with people I've met more recently — people I find interesting, who I want to get to know better. The idea is to learn more about each other, and to enjoy each other's company." So she gives impromptu suppers, with table decorations that change according to the time of year, using flowers and fruits that are in season. Her open-plan kitchen, laid out around a central island, means that she can enjoy her guests to the full. "For me, preparing food for friends is all part and parcel of the pleasure of entertaining. And I like to join in the conversation while I'm about it. Sometimes I even lay out a buffet in the kitchen and guests come and help themselves." Caroline Sarkozy's cuisine is simple and unpretentious but full of flavor, sometimes including dishes from her Middle Eastern childhood. "It's not necessarily the cooking that takes the most time, but rather driving all over Paris in search of good bread here, mature cheeses there, vegetables somewhere else. When it comes to quality I refuse to compromise." As could also be said of the objects with which she surrounds herself.

FACING PAGE
Caroline Sarkozy in the living room of her
Rive Gauche home on the banks of the Seine.

ABOVE AND FACING PAGE
On the left, a chair by André Arbus at the top of the entrance steps. On the right, in the entrance hall, a buffet by Ernst Spolén holds lamps designed by Paul Laszlo and made by Sito Lindberg, two bowls by Alev Ebüzziya Siesbye, and a jardinière by Gustave Serrurier-Bovy.

PAGES 254–255
In the living room, between a vintage sofa and a pair of armchairs that were flea-market finds, a coffee table designed by Hubert le Gall.

PAGE 256
The central island with marble top glimpsed through arches in the kitchen.

PAGE 257
A floral-themed table decoration, with Barbotine-ware candlesticks, embroidered tablecloth, budding hyacinths, and posies of flowers.

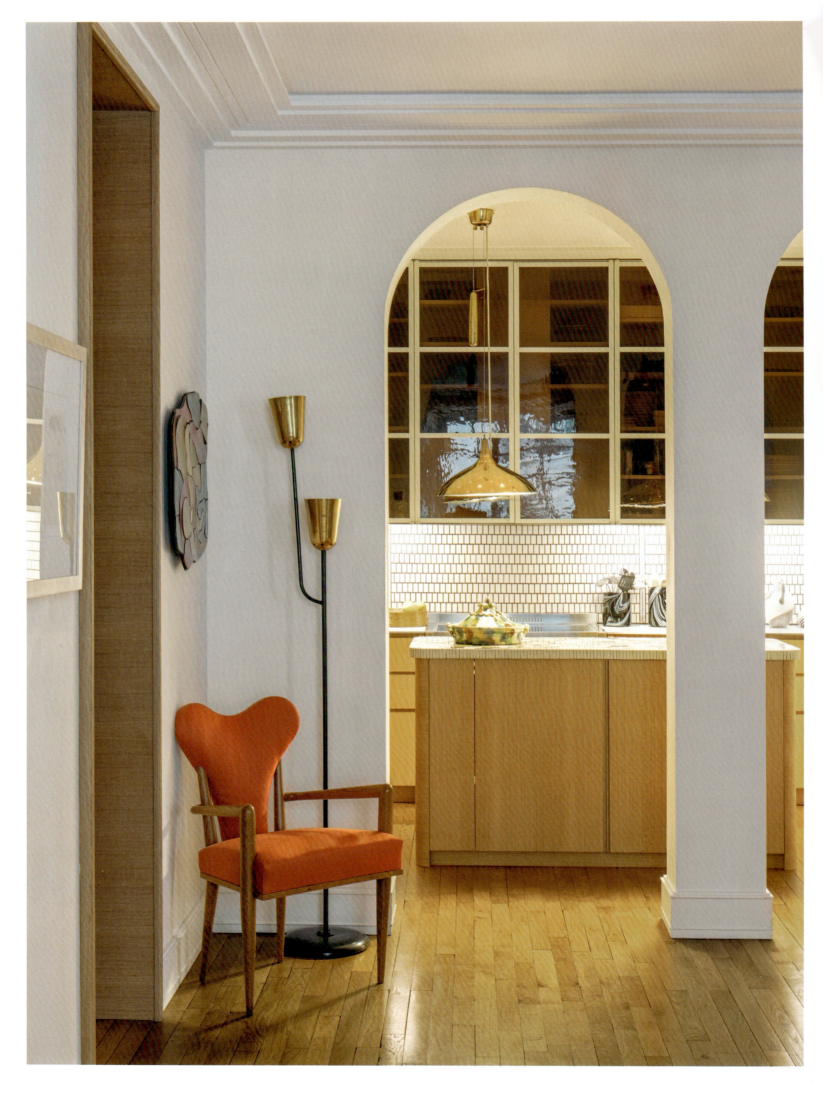

Cured Salmon with Gravlax Sauce and Ratte du Touquet Potatoes

Ingredients (serves 6)

FOR THE CURED SALMON
1 lb. 2 oz. (500 g) salmon fillet
3 tbsp olive oil
Juice of ½ lemon
1 small bunch fresh dill
2 tbsp cilantro
1 tbsp pink peppercorns
Black pepper

FOR THE GRAVLAX SAUCE
3 tbsp Dijon mustard
2 tbsp white vinegar
2 tbsp rapeseed oil
2 tbsp honey
2 bunches dill
Salt and white pepper

FOR THE RATTE DU TOUQUET POTATOES
2 lb. 3 oz. (1 kg) Ratte du Touquet potatoes
1 ½ tbsp (¾ oz./20 g) salted butter
Salt

Method

To cure the salmon, remove the skin from the fillet, then cut the flesh into slices ¼ in. (5 mm) thick.

In a bowl, mix the olive oil, ¼ of the lemon juice (not all of it or it will cook the salmon), chopped dill, cilantro, and pink peppercorns. Season with pepper.

Arrange the salmon slices in a shallow dish and cover them with the marinade. Cover the dish with aluminum foil and set aside in the refrigerator for at least 4 hours.

Remove from the refrigerator 1 hour before serving. Add the remaining lemon juice and transfer to a serving dish.

To make the gravlax sauce, beat the mustard and vinegar until they emulsify, add the oil and honey and continue beating. Mix in the dill and season with salt and pepper.

Set aside in a cool place for at least 4 hours. The gravlax sauce will keep for at least 4 days.

To prepare the potatoes, put them, unpeeled, in a saucepan and cover them with cold, salted water. Bring to the boil and simmer over a medium heat, half-covered, for 25 minutes. To serve, dot with salted butter.

To ensure the potatoes all cook at the same time, make sure they are all of similar size, or remove the smaller ones until the larger ones have cooked. You can prepare the potatoes in advance, and just before serving heat them for 2 minutes in the microwave, adding more salted butter.

• *Tip from Caroline* •
Crustarmor Gravlax Sauce, available from good fishmongers and online, is delicious.

Pia's Apple and Pear Gâteau

Ingredients (serves 6)

FOR THE GÂTEAU
1 lb. 2 oz. (500 g) Reinette apples
1 lb. 2 oz. (500 g) pears
Juice of 1 lemon
1 egg
1 cup (7 oz./200 g) superfine sugar
½ stick (2 oz./55 g) softened butter
    + a little more for greasing the mold
    and dotting the gâteau
Scant ½ cup (100 ml) whole milk
1 cup (5 ¼ oz./150 g) flour
Scant ½ cup (100 ml) Marsala
1 tbsp baking powder
3 pinches ground cinnamon
Pinch salt

FOR THE FRUIT COULIS
1 lb. 2 oz. (500 g) strawberries or raspberries
1 tbsp lemon juice
3 tbsp demerara sugar

Method

Preheat the oven to 375°F (175°C/Gas Mark 5).

Peel, core, and slice the apples and pears, then mix them with the lemon juice to prevent them from oxidizing. Set aside.

In a blender, blitz the egg, ¾ cup (5 ½ oz./150 g) of the superfine sugar, salt, and softened butter for 20 seconds.

Add the milk, sift in the flour, and add the Marsala, and blend for an additional 20 seconds. The mixture should be smooth, creamy, and semi-liquid in consistency.

Add the baking powder and blend for an additional 10 seconds.

Pour the mixture into a 9 in. (23–24 cm) mold, buttered and floured. Arrange circles of the apple and pear slices on top of the mixture. Sprinkle evenly with the rest of the sugar and the cinnamon, then dot with small knobs of butter.

Bake in the oven for 40 minutes.

To remove the gâteau from the mold, allow it to cool, carefully loosen the sides from the mold, and turn it upside down on to a flat plate.

To make the fruit coulis, add hulled strawberries or raspberries with the lemon juice and demerara sugar in a saucepan and cook over a low heat for 10 minutes, or until the fruit has released its juices. Blend the mixture, then sieve to remove the seeds. Allow to cool.

Serve the gâteau with the fruit coulis.

PAGES 262–263
In the bedroom, the bed was designed by Caroline Sarkozy and the pair of banquette seats by Otto Schulz. On the bedside tables by Gustave Serrurier-Bovy are ceramic lamps by Marc du Plantier.

Pierre Sauvage

He adores his friends, so he loves to entertain them and enjoy their company. Pierre Sauvage runs the Casa Lopez brand, as well as presiding over Tissus Choisis par Casa Lopez. This Paris showroom is dedicated to fabrics by designers who are a rare presence on the French market—like-minded souls such as Carolina Irving and Franz Potisek.

While his three shih tzus are his constant companions, his also shares his new home in the Perche region of Normandy with eleven horses, two donkeys, three pigs, twenty English hens, a flock of geese, and some fifty pheasants. An inveterate animal-lover, he has no time for hunting, which is best not mentioned in his presence. After twenty years in press and public relations with Christian Dior and Jean-Charles de Castelbajac, and as associate director of an agency specializing in luxury goods, Pierre Sauvage took over Casa Lopez in 2014. "I've always loved the label for its lightheartedness and its colorful Mediterranean style," he explains. "And I was familiar with its story." Through the strength of his conviction, Pierre Sauvage has transformed a carpet manufacturer into an all-embracing universe of everything for the home, offering not only tableware but also furniture, lighting, fragrances, and even illustrated decks of cards.

Over the years, the Parisian designer has invented a style unique to him, colorful, cheerful, and totally unpretentious. "I've always had constants in my various interiors, whether in my Paris apartment or my house in the Luberon: I like boldly patterned floors, strong colors, and prints on the walls. My idol is David Hicks, even if none of my homes comes close to his style." This is all true of his Normandy home, a Technicolor vision designed with his decorator friend Franz Potisek. Here, Pierre Sauvage loves to bring together family, old friends, and neighbors. "My modus operandi is always the same: a drink before the meal, with nibbles in place of starters, followed by just one course at the table. An Indian *kitchari*, bœuf bourguignon, perhaps a *blanquette de veau*—dishes that are simple and generous. I don't like spending ages over a meal!" He makes sure every occasion is a feast for the eyes as well, devoting great care to creating witty and fun table settings for every meal.

"The principle I adopt is to start off from one feature—it could be the dish I'm serving, a flower arrangement, or the tablecloth—and compose around it. You need to have a few different table services and a fair number of glasses to do this, admittedly; but nowadays, between Zara Home, flea markets, and eBay, you can find a whole range of things at reasonable prices. All you have to do is mix and match. The old rules don't really apply any more—now it's all about enjoyment. Why not strew your tablecloth with seashells? Or use semiprecious stones as knife rests? Or ramekins as vases? The important thing is to have fun!"

FACING PAGE
Pierre Sauvage in the grounds of his estate, preparing to mount Jupiter, his Spanish thoroughbred.

PAGES 266–267
The west façade of the nineteenth-century château.

ABOVE
A shady avenue in the grounds, beside the paddock where the thoroughbreds run free.

FACING PAGE
A dormer window with pediment and columns punctuates the slate roof.

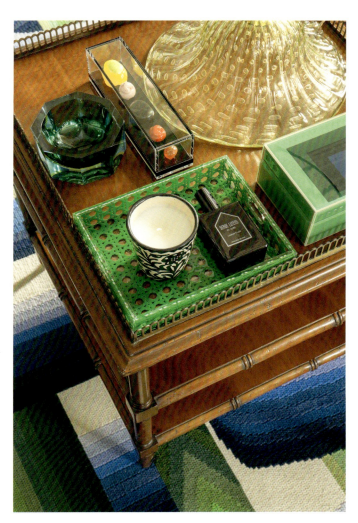

FACING PAGE
In the Adam-style entrance hall with Wedgwood-green walls, a table is laid with a cloth from Tissus Choisis par Casa Lopez.

ABOVE AND PAGES 272–273
The neoclassical grand salon, painted in vibrant green.

ABOVE
Shelves filled with a collection of tableware, including glasses from Murano and others painted by hand.

FACING PAGE
An antique faience collection on the wall of the telephone room.

FACING PAGE AND BELOW
The table is laid with Impératrice plates by Casa Lopez. The flowers were picked from the gardens.

Haddock Kedgeree

Ingredients (serves 6)

1 cup (9 oz./250 g) basmati rice
1 ¾ lb. (800 g) haddock
4 cups (1 l) milk
1 bay leaf
3 cloves garlic
3 onions
⅔ stick (2 ½ oz./75 g) butter
2 generous tbsp curry powder
1 bottle white wine
2 organic lemons, 1 juiced and 1 sliced
1 large bunch cilantro
Salt and freshly ground black pepper

Method

Rince the rice, drain, and set aside.

In a casserole dish, poach the haddock with the milk and bay leaf for 10 minutes over a low heat. Drain, flake, and set aside.

Finely chop the garlic and onions and sauté them in the butter with 2 generous tablespoons of curry powder. Season with salt and pepper. Add the rice and cook for 2–3 minutes, until pearly and translucent.

Gradually add the white wine, then cook the rice while stirring, as for a risotto.

When the rice is cooked, add the flaked haddock and lemon juice and mix together.

Arrange in a shallow serving dish and cover with chopped cilantro and slices of lemon.

RIGHT
Cauliflower florets with olive oil and aromatic plants.

Chocolate Mousse

Ingredients (serves 6)

2 cups (500 ml) heavy cream
5 ¼ oz. (150 g) 70% bitter chocolate
5 egg yolks
⅔ cup (4 ½ oz./125 g) superfine sugar
⅔ stick (2 ½ oz./75 g) butter, softened
2 tbsp cocoa powder
Pinch salt

Method

Refrigerate the cream for several hours until well chilled.
Place the bowl for whipping the cream in the freezer for 1 hour.

Pour the chilled cream into the chilled bowl and add a small pinch of salt.
Whip the cream with an electric whisk to medium peaks.
Set aside in the refrigerator.

Melt the chocolate in a bain-marie.

Boil water for a second bain-marie.

Meanwhile, in a bowl, use an electric whisk to beat the egg yolks with the superfine sugar and softened butter until pale and smooth.

Place the bowl containing the egg, sugar, and butter mixture in the second bain-marie, away from the heat, and whisk for 10 minutes with the electric whisk, until the mixture has doubled in volume.
Remove the bowl from the bain-marie.

Mix the melted chocolate into the egg, sugar, and butter mixture, then gradually add the cocoa powder. Mix well with a spatula.
Using the spatula, very gently fold in the whipped cream.

Pour the mousse into ramekins or a large bowl.

Chill in the refrigerator for at least 2–3 hours before serving.

RIGHT, TOP AND BOTTOM
One of the arches on the piano nobile, and a Chinese ceramic lion keeping watch over the kitchen stoves.

FACING PAGE
A Gothic Revival lantern hangs above the main staircase, adding a nineteenth-century touch that is echoed by the pink opaline lamps placed on the console table.

FACING PAGE
The canopy over the bed is lit by a nineteenth-century lamp in Andalusian style.

ABOVE, LEFT
A pair of Napoleon III-style pouffes designed by Madeleine Castaing standing on a Russian carpet.

ABOVE, RIGHT
The mirror on the marble fireplace reflecting the room's painted woodwork.

286 Pierre Sauvage **How They Entertain**

RIGHT
A nocturnal view of the nineteenth-century façade of the château, added to the seventeenth-century residence and medieval tower in 1846.

Scott Stover

American-born Scott Stover divides his time between Los Angeles and deepest Provence. Enticed to the Luberon by a major affair of the heart, once there he also succumbed to the delights of the landscapes and purchased a traditional manor house, around which his partner, the landscape architect Philippe Cottet, laid out a stunning contemporary garden.

For a long time, Paris was his base. After studying semiotics and history of art at Columbia University in New York, he pursued a career in banking, and then in 2005 founded his own philanthropy advisory firm. Since then, he has led projects in the United States, Europe, and Asia, working with clients ranging from public institutions to private foundations and artist foundations. So it is only natural that he should have works by Thomas Ruff and James Welling on the walls of the manor house, testifying to his interest in conceptual photography. Minimalist in spirit, the interior design of this fine seventeenth-century building is imbued with a rigorous elegance. Armchairs by Philippe Hurel (1955), Christian Liaigre coffee table and sofa (1943–2020), and a Mies van der Rohe banquette seating (1886–1969) contribute to the modernist spirit of these resolutely masculine interiors.

This desire for a life in tune with contemporary design is also reflected in the building's surroundings. "I wanted the garden to be as beautiful in winter as in summer," says Scott Stover. "In Provence the weather's good all year round. So this is not a flower garden but a topiary garden, laid out around twelve different outdoor spaces—including an open-air salon—illustrating the different stages of life, from youth to the age of wisdom. Strolling through it is a kind of rite of passage." Leading from the wildness of untamed nature to the rigorous order of box topiary, the walk takes over an hour.

The Italian inspiration behind the garden at La Chabaude, created by Philippe Cottet from the 2000s, echoes the history of the site, which lay on the ancient Roman road between Italy and Spain. The garden lies open to the hills and valleys of the surrounding maquis, and in its planting, featuring a range of Mediterranean shrubs and plants, it echoes this landscape. "In summer, depending on the weather, we tend to entertain in the garden: we serve aperitifs in one spot, sit down to eat at a round table in another, and finish off with a tisane under the boughs of the ancient oak trees while gazing out over the view. We usually have small, intimate gatherings of four or six people. Although my godson and goddaughter, who have been coming here since they were children, both got married here, which I found very touching; there were many more of us then, and they were wonderfully festive occasions."

FACING PAGE
The Franco-American art collector Scott Stover commissioned the landscape designer Philippe Cottet to create a dry garden of austere elegance and restraint but also full of life.

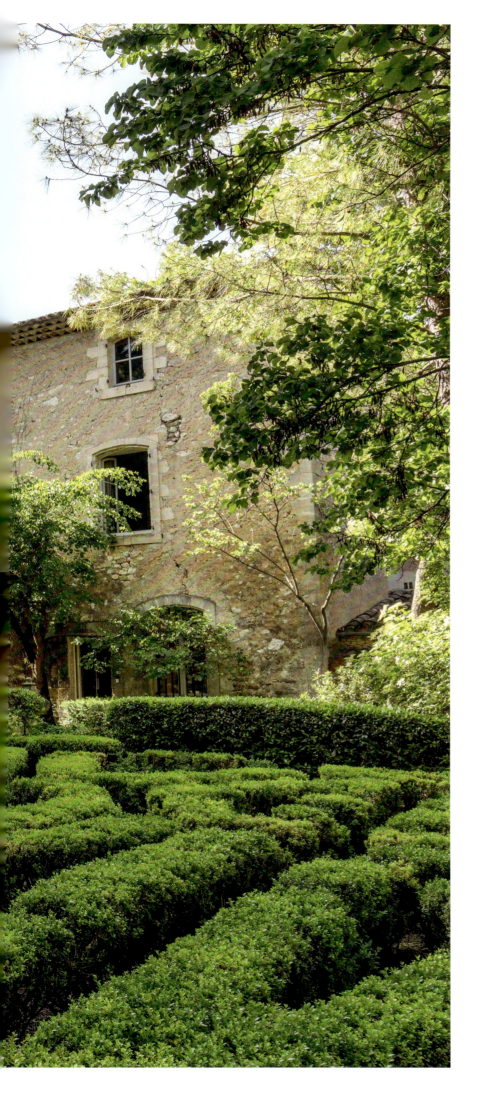

LEFT
Beneath the stone walls of the Provençal house, the landscape designer Philippe Cottet designed a clipped box parterre, like an abstract maze that leads the eye to infinity.

LEFT, ABOVE, AND FACING PAGE
Outdoor living spaces and pools, steps and water features punctuate a bucolic stroll through the gardens, designed by Philippe Cottet as a sort of rite of passage.

FACING PAGE
Rigorous restraint is the hallmark of the dining space, with wrought-iron chairs and lantern surrounding a minimalist stone table.

ABOVE
A detail of the leafy table decoration.

Light Eton Mess

Ingredients (serves 4)

FOR THE CRÈME CHANTILLY
2 cups (500 ml) heavy cream
¼ cup (1¼ oz./35 g) confectioners' sugar

FOR THE MERINGUE
½ cup (3½ oz./100 g) superfine sugar
2 egg whites

FOR THE BASE AND GARNISH
¾ cup (7 oz./200 g) Greek yogurt
Scant ½ cup (3½ oz./100 g) raspberry purée
9 oz. (250 g) mixed red fruits (strawberries, raspberries, blueberries, blackberries)

Method

To make the crème chantilly, refrigerate the cream and the bowl for whipping until both are both well chilled. Pour the cream into the bowl and add the confectioners' sugar.

Whip the mixture with an electric whisk, gradually increasing the speed every 30 seconds or so. Allow to rest in the refrigerator for at least 2 hours before serving.

To make the meringue, preheat the oven to 225°F (110°C/Gas Mark ¼).

At least 15 minutes beforehand, remove the eggs from the refrigerator. Separate the whites of the eggs into a deep bowl, ensuring there are no traces of yolk. Add a pinch of salt and with an electric whisk whip into stiff peaks, adding the sugar gradually as you continue to beat.

Place a sheet of parchment paper on a baking tray and dot it with little meringues. Bake in the oven for an hour.

Remove from the oven and allow to cool on a rack.

Take a large bowl or 4 individual bowls, spoon in a layer of Greek yogurt and top with the raspberry purée. Cover with crème chantilly.

Top with the mixed red fruits and cooled meringues to serve.

PAGES 298–299
The passage leading to the staircase offers a glimpse of banquette seating filling the width of a gently curving alcove.

PAGES 300–301
The living room features contemporary furniture and a hand-woven Berber rug.

ABOVE
The wrought-iron stair rail adds a further note of elegant simplicity.

FACING PAGE
A Christian Liaigre chair sits in the library adjoining the main bedroom.

Sabine Van Vlaenderen Badinter

While she now devotes her time and energy to the Fondation de la Vocation, a social enterprise to support young people in their vocational training, for many years Sabine Van Vlaenderen Badinter exercised her skills in the field of interior design. The interiors of her tasteful Paris home bear witness to her talents and reflect her quest for calm and tranquility.

Perhaps it is her Belgian background, a certain Flemish rigor, that dictates the Parisienne's neutral palette of shades of greige, powder gray, and off-white. Sabine Van Vlaenderen Badinter's beautiful Left Bank apartment epitomizes elegance in simplicity. Her furniture reflects the neoclassical restraint characteristic of the great designers of the 1940s, led by Paul Dupré-Lafon (1900–1971) and Guglielmo Ulrich (1904–1977). "I like furniture that emanates a certain strength, arranged in spaces that are not too busy; you have to leave room for life, not clutter yourself up with objects or souvenirs," she says. The same applies to her unassuming style of entertaining. What Sabine Van Vlaenderen Badinter enjoys most are cozy dinners with friends in her kitchen. Sometimes, when she has more guests, she likes to set a pretty table in her dining room. "I take a great deal of care over it, and I appreciate a certain elegance, but I would hate my flower arrangements to dominate the conversation. My friends have better things to talk about!" The same goes for the fuss-free dishes she serves: "I'm not looking to be a great chef!"

Sabine Van Vlaenderen Badinter's calling is to enable disadvantaged young people in forging their own futures. Five years ago, Élisabeth Badinter, president of the Fondation de la Vocation and mother of Benjamin Badinter, Sabine's partner, asked her to join her in this philanthropic family venture, started in 1959 by Marcel Bleustein-Blanchet (1906–1996). Every year, it supports successful applicants aged between eighteen and thirty by awarding them a bursary to help them bring a professional project to fruition. It could be to pay for studies, for accommodation for training abroad, or even for the indispensable tools of their trade. Some of them have an ambition to become bakers, others to be musicians or even astrophysicists.

Sabine Van Vlaenderen Badinter is responsible for the foundation and its partnerships. In this kind of venture, progress can only be made with supportive partners. So if this appeals, why not follow your heart and sponsor a budding talent!

FACING PAGE
Sabine Van Vlaenderen Badinter in her Rive Gauche apartment, with its view over a shady garden that formerly belonged to Pierre Berger.

PAGES 306–307
The conservatory, with its pair of Otto Schulz armchairs.

RIGHT
The main living room, with its Directoire architecture picked out in a palette of whites.

ABOVE
An Austrian 1930s Lauscha Bimini liqueur and champagne set in colored crystal and *pâte de verre*.

FACING PAGE
A collection of glassware displayed in a 1950s Italian bookcase repurposed as dresser shelves.

FACING PAGE AND BELOW
Instead of one large flower arrangement, the table is decorated with a succession of smaller ones.

RIGHT
On the wall, a painting by the Japanese artist Nobuo Sekine is flanked by a pair of plaster wall sconces by Patrice Dangel, who also designed the ceiling light.

Zucchini, Petits Pois, and Basil Velouté

Ingredients (serves 6–8)

1/3 cup (75 ml) olive oil
2–3 cloves garlic
6 zucchini (around 2 3/4 lb./1.3 kg)
4 cups (1 l) vegetable stock
1 lb. 2 oz. (500 g) petits pois (fresh or frozen)
1 3/4 oz. (50 g) fresh basil
7 oz. (200 g) feta
Pinch flaked almonds, to decorate
1 tsp lemon zest
Salt and freshly ground black pepper

Method

In a stewpot, heat the olive oil over a medium–high heat. Sauté the whole garlic cloves for 2–3 minutes until golden. Add the zucchini sliced in 1 in. (3 cm) rounds, 1 teaspoon of salt and pepper to taste, and cook for 3 minutes, stirring constantly.

When the zucchini starts to color, cover it with the vegetable stock and add water if necessary. Bring to the boil and cook for 7 minutes, until the zucchini is soft but still nice and green.

Add the petits pois and cook for 10 minutes, then add the basil. Remove from the heat immediately. If there is too much liquid, remove some before blending to adjust the consistency, and blend with a blender or stick blender. Rapid blending helps to fix the bright green color of the velouté.

Pour the velouté into individual bowls or ramekins, then sprinkle with the crumbled feta, flaked almonds, and lemon zest.

If liked, finish with black pepper and a drizzle of olive oil. Serve immediately.

Stuffed Tomatoes and Zucchini

Ingredients (serves 6–8)

12 small tomatoes
8 small round zucchini
Salt

FOR THE STUFFING

2 tbsp olive oil, plus extra for drizzling
2 onions, finely chopped
1 clove garlic, finely chopped
2 cans peeled tomatoes, drained and deseeded
12 chard leaves, green part sliced
7 oz. (200 g) salt pork or pancetta, chopped
7 oz. (200 g) ground beef
7 oz. (200 g) ground veal
10 sprigs basil
Generous 1 cup (3 1/2 oz./100 g) grated Parmesan
2 eggs, beaten
Salt and freshly ground black pepper

FOR THE SAUCE

Olive oil, for sautéing
1 onion, finely chopped
1 large can peeled tomatoes
Rosemary
Thyme
Bay leaf
Salt and freshly ground black pepper

Method

Slice the tops off the tomatoes and zucchini and set aside. Carefully remove the seeds from the tomatoes and zucchini and hollow out the insides, then sprinkle them with salt. Allow to sit for 10 minutes, then place them upside down on an oven shelf or rack to drain the water from inside.

Meanwhile, make the stuffing: heat 2 tablespoons of olive oil in a stewpot and add the finely chopped onions and garlic, 2 cans peeled tomatoes, sliced chard leaves, chopped salt pork or pancetta, and ground beef and veal. Finally, add the basil leaves. Cook over a medium heat for around 15 minutes, then allow to cool.

Preheat the oven to 450°F (210°C/Gas Mark 8).

Add the Parmesan and beaten eggs to the stuffing mixture. Mix well and season with salt and pepper.

Fill the tomatoes and zucchini with the stuffing and arrange them in a lightly oiled dish. Drizzle with olive oil. Bake in the oven for around 45 minutes.

Meanwhile, make the sauce. Heat a little olive oil in a saucepan and sauté the onion. Add the peeled tomatoes, rosemary, thyme, and bay leaf. Season with salt and pepper. Cook for 45 minutes, until smooth.

Serve the tomatoes and zucchini with the sauce separately.

BELOW
View into the conservatory.

FACING PAGE
On the desk stand a ceramic lamp by George Jouves and a Nordic modernist sculpture.

Index of Recipes

Starters
Endive Salad with Roquefort and Walnuts *170*
Lemon Garlic Shrimp *230*
"Le Floreless" Cocktail *94*
Russian Salad *17*
Sealed Scallops *187*
Shrimp Cocktail *215*
Soupe au Potimarron (Squash Soup) *34*
Zucchini, Petits Pois, and Basil Velouté *315*

Main Courses
Blanquette de Veau *79*
Cured Salmon with Gravlax Sauce
 and Ratte du Touquet Potatoes *258*
Fresh Tomato and Garlic Pasta *170*
Gratin of Baby Vegetables with Goat Cheese *122*
Haddock Kedgeree *279*
Kim's Argentinian *Hachis Parmentier* (Shepherd's Pie) *187*
Leek Quiche with Flowers *34*
Potato Gâteau *136*
Provençale Tart with Tapenade *112*
Red Lentil Dhal with Spinach and Coconut Milk *158*
Roast Chicken *242*
Sea Bass Ceviche *46*
Shoulder of Lamb *à la Provençale* *215*
Stuffed Tomatoes and Zucchini *315*
Veal Loaf, Carrots, Heritage Vegetables,
 and Potatoes with Rosemary *201*

Desserts
Almond and Honey Tart *188*
Baked Alaska *216*
Chocolate Mousse *280*
Fruit Crumble *140*
Green Apple Tart with Lemon Verbena Sugar *125*
Îles Flottantes (Floating Islands) *82*
Indian Coconut Custard with Passion Fruit *161*
Light Eton Mess *296*
Orange and Mint Salad *50*
Pia's Apple and Pear Gâteau *261*
Rhubarb and Strawberry Meringue Pie *94*
Tiramisu *64*
Ultra-Creamy Chocolate Cream *188*
Vanilla Ice Cream and Hot Fudge Sauce *245*

Acknowledgments

Pierre Sauvage would like to thank Filipa de Abreu, Aurélie Bidermann, Isabelle de Borchgrave, Sophie Bouilhet-Dumas, Muriel Brandolini, Flore de Brantes, Brigitte Bury Dervault, Maurice Dervault, Françoise Dumas, Nathalie Farman-Farma, Laura Gonzalez, Olympia and Ariadne Irving, Isabelle Moltzer, Pascale Mussard, Franz Potisek, Rebecca de Ravenel, Remy Renzullo, Caroline Sarkozy, Scott Stover, Sabine Van Vlaenderen Badinter, Carolina Irving, Cédric Saint André Perrin, Ambroise Tézenas, Guillaume de Seynes, Mario Tavella, Victoria Ducluzeau, Emma Mascandola, Suzanne Tise-Isoré, Bernard Lagacé and Cécile Baribaud.

Photographic Credits

t: top, b: bottom, l: left, r: right

All photographs in this book were taken by Ambroise Tézenas.

P. 28: © Claude Lalanne/Adagp, Paris, 2024 (sculpture); p. 28: © Zao Wou-Ki/Adagp, Paris, 2024 (watercolor); p. 31: © Jacques Adnet/Adagp, Paris, 2024 (wardrobe); p. 151: © Laurent Dufour/Adagp, Paris, 2024 (bas-relief); pp. 154, 155tr, 155b, 156–157: © Fabienne l'Hostis/Adagp, Paris, 2024 (table); pp. 196–197, 199, 200 : © Christian Astuguevieille/Adagp, Paris, 2024 (chairs, armchairs, temple); p. 199: © Erede Ettore Sottsass/Adagp, Paris, 2024 (pepper mill); p. 205tl: © Julio Villani/Adagp, Paris, 2024 (sculpture); pp. 218–219: © Brigitte Terziev Najovits/Adagp, Paris, 2024 (candlesticks and lamps); p. 252l, 253: © Arbus/Adagp, Paris, 2024 (chair); pp. 254–255: © Hubert le Gall/Adagp, Paris, 2024 (coffee table); p. 256: © Jean Royère Estate/Adagp, Paris, 2024 (armchair); pp. 300–301: © Ludwig Mies Van Der Rohe/Adagp, Paris, 2024 (banquette seating); pp. 312–313: © Martin Szekely/Adagp, Paris, 2024 (table); p. 313tr: © Paul Dupré-Lafon/Adagp, Paris, 2024 (chairs); back covers: © Christian Astuguevieille/Adagp, Paris, 2024 (chairs, armchairs, temple).

Every effort has been made to identify copyright holders of the images reproduced in this book. Any errors or omissions referred to the publisher will be corrected in subsequent printings.

Editorial direction
Suzanne Tise-Isoré
Style & Design Collection

Editorial coordination
Cécile Baribaud

Graphic design
Bernard Lagacé

Translated from the French by
Barbara Mellor

Copy editing and proofreading
Lindsay Porter

Production
Élodie Conjat

Color separation
Les Artisans du Regard, Paris

Printed by
Indice, Spain

Simultaneously published in French
as *Plans de table: Quand recevoir est un art*
© Éditions Flammarion, Paris, 2024

English-language edition
© Éditions Flammarion, Paris, 2024

All rights reserved. No part of this publication may be reproduced in any from or any means, electronic, photocopy, information retrieval system or otherwise, without written permission from Éditions Flammarion.

Éditions Flammarion
82, Rue Saint Lazare
75009 Paris

editions.flammarion.com
@styleanddesignflammarion
@flammarioninternational

24 25 26 3 2 1
ISBN: 978-2-08-044056-3
Legal Deposit: 10/2024